LATIMER PUBLICATIONS

The Genius of George Whitefield

Reflections on his Ministry from 21st Century Africa

BENJAMIN DEAN AND ADRIAAN C. NEELE (EDITORS)
WITH A PREFACE BY THOMAS S. KIDD

The Latimer Trust

The Genius of George Whitefield: Reflections on his Ministry from 21st Century Africa© The Latimer Trust 2015

ISBN 978-1-906327-37-8

Cover photo: Antique Map 1755© Sergey Kamshylin - Fotolia.com

Published by the Latimer Trust December 2015

The Latimer Trust (formerly Latimer House, Oxford) is a conservative Evangelical research organisation within the Church of England, whose main aim is to promote the history and theology of Anglicanism as understood by those in the Reformed tradition. Interested readers are welcome to consult its website for further details of its many activities.

The Latimer Trust
London N14 4PS UK
Registered Charity: 1084337
Company Number: 4104465
Web: www.latimertrust.org
E-mail: administrator@latimertrust.org

Views expressed in works published by The Latimer Trust are those of the authors and do not necessarily represent the official position of The Latimer Trust.

'Whitefield was a born actor, a born-again orator, and a tireless evangelistic preacher with a huge, heart-warming voice, a huge intensity as a communicator, and a grand strategy for making Christ known on both sides of the Atlantic. He undoubtedly was the best known, most widely heard, and most effective spokesman for the Saviour all through the thirty-plus years of his public ministry. Happily this Symposium, scholarly and sympathetic, sponsored by George Whitefield College in Cape Town, goes far towards doing him justice on his 300th anniversary'
(J. I. Packer, Board of Governors' Professor of Theology at Regent College in Vancouver, British Columbia and theologian emeritus of the Anglican Church in North America).

'George Whitefield is such a significant figure in the making of Evangelicalism, that he deserves far more study than he has received. This book makes a first class introduction to the issues which rightly catch our attention'
(Archbishop Peter Jensen, General Secretary of GAFCON).

'Whitefield's outstanding (if imperfect) ministry displayed a life lived in relentless passion for God's Kingdom. This timely review urges similar faithfulness to biblical truth in our own day'
(Archbishop Emmanuel Egbunu, Diocese of Lokoja, Nigeria).

'Alas, we cannot re-live (and perhaps now can scarcely imagine) what Whitefield's hearers experienced. But the matter of his preaching, his Calvinistic evangelicalism, can be revisited. This impressive book will help us to become more acquainted both with this remarkable man, and with his message.'
(Paul Helm, formerly Professor of the History and Philosophy of Religion, King's College, London).

'Prior to reading this delightful collection I was one of those evangelical Anglicans unaccountably ignorant of the full extent of Whitefield's significance. Thankfully, that gap has now been filled! This collection presents a compelling picture of a great and complex man, giving the novice reader an introduction to his life and the more advanced reader insight into his theology and practice. I warmly recommend it.'
(John Yates III, Rector of Holy Trinity Anglican Church, Raleigh, North Carolina).

CONTENTS

Acknowledgements i

Contributors ii

Preface *by Thomas S. Kidd* iii

1. George Whitefield — the Anglican Evangelist *by Lee Gatiss*......1
   - 1.1. Positively Anglican..1
   - 1.2. The Anglican Doctrine of the Indwelling Spirit 3
   - 1.3. Anglican Cavalryman..6
   - 1.4. Facing opposition from Anglican authorities.......................8
   - 1.5. An Anglican Evangelical Criticism of Whitefield...............11
   - 1.6. Conclusion 13
   - 1.7. Sources..13

2. George Whitefield and Preached Calvinism *by Melvin Tinker*...........15
   - 2.1. Introduction 15
   - 2.2. Which Calvinism?...16
   - 2.3. An Authentic or Opportunistic Calvinist?.........................19
   - 2.4. Preached Calvinism 22
   - 2.5. Conclusion 28
   - 2.6. Sources..30

3. The Pastoral Sermons of George Whitefield
   by Victor Emma-Adamah and Phumezo Masango 31
   - 3.1. George Whitefield as 'Pastor'?..31
   - 3.2. Introduction 31
   - 3.3. 'The one thing needful': the care of souls as paradigm for Whitefield's 'pastoral' ministry...35
   - 3.4. Aspects of Whitefield's sermons as pastoral......................38
   - 3.5. Conclusion 48
   - 3.6. Sources..49

4. Whitefield's Evangelical Theology *by Benjamin Dean*................51
   - 4.1. Original sin 55
   - 4.2. Eternal judgment..59
   - 4.3. Justification by faith: forgiveness and acceptance 62
   - 4.4. Regeneration: the new birth 68
   - 4.5. Conclusion 73
   - 4.6. Afterword: Whitefield and slavery 73
   - 4.7. Sources..76

5. George Whitefield and Africa: Personal Reflections
   by David Seccombe 79
5.1. *What can we learn then from this remarkable man?* 83
5.2. *Sources* 85

6. George Whitefield and Revival: Scotland 1741-42 *by Ian J. Shaw* 87
6.1. *The nature of revival* 90
6.2. *The Evangelical revival background* 92
6.3. *George Whitefield's ministry before 1741-42* 92
6.4. *Revival in eighteenth-century Scotland* 95
6.5. *The Sermons* 99
6.6. *Opposition* 104
6.7. *Assessment* 105
6.8. *Sources* 108

7. The Meeting of Jonathan Edwards and George Whitefield
   by Adriaan C. Neele 111
7.1. *Introduction* 111
7.2. *Edwards and Whitefield: Background* 113
7.3. *Edwards and Whitefield: Meeting* 115
7.4. *Edwards and Whitefield: Hearing of the Word* 116
7.5. *Conclusion* 122
7.6. *Sources* 123

8. Conference Closing Prayer *by Ross Anderson* 125

Acknowledgements

The essays contained in this volume originated as lectures delivered in August 2014 during 'The Whitefield Symposium' held at George Whitefield College, Cape Town, in partnership with Jonathan Edwards Centre Africa, to commemorate the 300th Anniversary of Whitefield's birth. Special thanks are due to the Principal and Board of GWC for sponsoring this event, as well as to Nevil Carrington, Sigrid Holscher, and Alison Lee for their thoughtful planning and excellent organization, which did so much to make the Symposium successful and enjoyable. The editors are deeply grateful to the Symposium speakers for their tremendous participation during several happy days together and for their fine contributions to the now published version of proceedings. Thanks and appreciation is due also to Gerald Bray for his kind help with publication, and to Thomas Kidd for supplying the Preface.

*****

This work is dedicated to the students, faculty, and staff of George Whitefield College, Cape Town, and to the students and faculty of Jonathan Edwards Centre Africa, Bloemfontein, ministers of the Lord Jesus Christ. May Almighty God our Father continue this good work of training for Gospel service throughout the world, by the help of his Holy Spirit, producing love, knowledge, and all discernment, for the salvation of many at the day of Christ. To whom be all glory and praise.

Contributors

Ross Anderson is John Stott Lecturer in Bible and Ministry at George Whitefield College, Cape Town.

Benjamin Dean is Lecturer in Systematic Theology and Dean of Postgraduate Studies at George Whitefield College, Cape Town.

Victor Emma-Adamah is a graduate of the Bible Institute of South Africa and the University of the Free State. He is commencing PhD studies in Philosophical Theology at the University of Cambridge.

Lee Gatiss is the Director of Church Society, Adjunct Lecturer in Church History at Wales Evangelical School of Theology, and Research Fellow of the Jonathan Edwards Centre Africa at the University of the Free State.

Thomas S. Kidd is Distinguished Professor of History at Baylor University and the author of books including *George Whitefield: America's Spiritual Founding Father* (2014).

Phumezo Masango, Rector of Christ Church, Khayelitsha, Cape Town, is joining the Faculty of George Whitefield College in early 2016.

Adriaan Neele serves as Research Scholar, and Digital Editor at the Jonathan Edwards Center at Yale University, and as Professor of Historical Theology and Director at the Jonathan Edwards Centre Africa at the University of the Free State.

David Seccombe is formerly Principal of George Whitefield College, Cape Town (1993-2012).

Ian J. Shaw is Honorary Fellow at the School of Divinity, New College, Edinburgh University, Director of the Langham UK Scholarship Programme, and Research Fellow of the Jonathan Edwards Centre Africa at the University of the Free State.

Melvin Tinker is Vicar of St John Newland, Kingston upon Hull.

Preface *by Thomas S. Kidd*

I am honoured to offer a preface to this excellent volume, which seeks to highlight the significance of the ministry of George Whitefield. As David Seccombe notes in his essay here, the first lesson for all Christians to learn from Whitefield's story is 'the power of the preached gospel, when God moves in mercy to open people's hearts by his Holy Spirit.' George Whitefield was a flawed vessel, as all mere mortals are, but through his evangelistic efforts and tireless zeal God worked wonders that took the Anglo-American world by storm.

Writings on George Whitefield have taken a twisting path since his death in 1770, a path that helps to account for his relative lack of notoriety in today's evangelical world. Although he was by far the best-known preacher in mid-eighteenth century Britain and America, he is now surpassed in fame by Jonathan Edwards and John Wesley. Our memory of Whitefield is hampered by the fact that the key to his success was his preaching *as delivered in the moment*. The eighteenth century, as a pre-electronic age, lacked microphones and video recording technology, so those sermons, as delivered, are lost to us. We can hear echoes in the testimonies of those who were there at his titanic field assemblies, and in the reports of 'the extraordinary Influence of his Oratory on his Hearers,' as the religious sceptic (and long-time friend of Whitefield) Benjamin Franklin put it.

By contrast, the brilliance of Jonathan Edwards remained in his sermons and treatises *as written*. Thus we can peruse the riches of his theological insights in *Religious Affections* and *The Freedom of the Will* and not lose much, if any, of their original impact. Similarly, the genius of Wesley was in organizing, so his institutional legacy lingered in the Methodist Church long after his death. For a century and more after his death, Christian admirers did continue to herald Whitefield's work and impact. But inevitably, memories of him faded. Elite academics, when they did remember him, tended to cast him as an anti-intellectual demagogue.

In the 1970s, a deep schism emerged in the study of Whitefield, in which devotional Christian and formal academic approaches to Whitefield entirely broke apart. It is a divide that has never seemed to mark the study of Edwards or Wesley in the same fundamental way. The split over Whitefield was occasioned by the publication of Arnold Dallimore's openly Christian two-volume biography of Whitefield, which remains the most thorough account of Whitefield's three decades of public ministry. Dallimore was a Canadian pastor writing the book in his spare time. His extensive labours, perceived as a distraction by some in his church, eventually led him to resign his pastorate before the second volume appeared. Academic historians, to the extent that they acknowledged Dallimore, did not respond well to his biography. Yale historian Jon Butler (who is also known for once denying that a 'Great Awakening' even happened) said that Dallimore's biography was 'thoroughly out of touch with modern scholarship and very much too long.' Butler's Yale colleague Harry Stout soon produced a biography of Whitefield, *The Divine Dramatist* (1991), which seemed to imply that Whitefield was all show and no substance. The preacher sold the 'New Birth,' Stout wrote, 'with all the dramatic artifice of a huckster.' Calvinist and evangelical pastors, including Dallimore, blasted Stout's portrayal of Whitefield. John Piper declared that Stout's Whitefield was 'the most sustained piece of historical cynicism I have ever read.' For at least forty years, divergent academic and devotional Christian approaches split the path of Whitefield histories into two widely separate branches.

Part of my aspiration in writing a new biography of Whitefield, 2014's *George Whitefield: America's Spiritual Founding Father*, was to bring a bit of healing to this rift. As an academic historian and an evangelical believer, I thought perhaps I might be able to bring the devotional and academic approaches to Whitefield back into conversation. I sought to write something that observes the usual conventions of academic history, including an awareness of the broader cultural context of Whitefield's Anglo-American society. But I also wanted to present a biography that Christians, especially church leaders, could receive as a critical but sympathetic study of the eighteenth-century's greatest evangelist.

One of my main priorities in the biography, one shared by the authors in this volume, was to paint a portrait of Whitefield as he saw himself: as forgiven sinner and an evangelical, Calvinist preacher. Another problem created by the divergence of the academic and pietistic approaches to Whitefield is that while the overtly Christian literature never forgot about Whitefield's primary spiritual identity, the academic work on Whitefield tended to emphasize themes such as Whitefield and theatre culture (Stout), or Whitefield and the emerging market economy, a thesis employed by Frank Lambert's *'Pedlar in Divinity': George Whitefield and the Transatlantic Revivals* (1994). Not that either of these themes are wrong – Whitefield's preaching excellence was undoubtedly enhanced by his background in the theatre. He also had an uncanny grasp of possibilities opened by the new media of his era (thus his business relationship with Philadelphia printer Benjamin Franklin). But the academic treatments had downplayed the core principles that made Whitefield tick. The door remained wide open for an academic biography that placed Whitefield in the 'fractious milieu' of the early evangelical movement.

My biography was timed for release in conjunction with Whitefield's 300th birthday in December 2014, a commemoration which also inspired a number of events across the globe, including the conference in Cape Town, South Africa, which produced this book of essays. Although Whitefield's renown will probably never return to the stratospheric heights it reached in the 1740s, these events and publications can only help us better remember him, and also to bridge the unfortunate divide between academic and pietistic biographies. One healthy aspect of the commemorations is that even the overtly Christian ones have been willing to admit Whitefield's manifest failings. They have not adopted an older model of Christian hagiography which might have felt compelled to present someone like Whitefield as a pristine saint. The greatest moral problem related to Whitefield's career was his entanglement in slavery and slave owning. As Benjamin Dean notes in an extended aside in his essay here, given the Cape Town seminar's 'location in postcolonial South Africa and Africa, it is particularly appropriate to register that our subject's complicity in and even advocacy of 'humane' chattel slavery remains reprehensible and problematic.'

What do we do when standard bearers for the Kingdom turn out to be flawed, and even sinful? Accounting for the failings of the heroes of church history is one of the greatest challenges to any Christian historian. We must navigate between two extreme kinds of reaction. One overreaction would be to contend that if Whitefield did not realize the moral enormities associated with slavery and the slave trade, then he is of no use to us today, and better forgotten rather than celebrated. The other extreme would be to take offense at anyone mentioning our hero's imperfections, as if the mere noting of them somehow denies that he was used by God. But as Whitefield himself suggested, it is better to be honest about the failings of figures in Christian history, and realize that God uses all of us in spite of our imperfections. Although he puts all of his true children on the path of sanctification, God does not wait for us to reach absolute holiness before employing us in the work of the Kingdom. If perfection was required for serving in God's Kingdom, then God would have a very short list of people with whom He could work. I suppose the only person who would qualify would be a certain carpenter's son from Nazareth.

Our admission of Whitefield's time-bound imperfections should not detract from our awe at the remarkable effects of his ministry. Untold thousands of people put their faith in Christ for the first time because of his preaching, and many thousands of others had their flagging faith renewed by hearing him speak or reading his voluminous writings. In a purely historical sense, it would be difficult to overstate Whitefield's significance. In his time, he was simply the most famous person in Britain and America. Admittedly, more people might have recognized the name of Britain's king (which in the 1740s was King George II). But far fewer had seen the king, or been influenced by anything the king said or wrote. British colonists in America especially felt Whitefield's massive effect on society. Whitefield made a remarkable seven visits to the American colonies. Doing so required dangerous and often interminable Atlantic Ocean voyages. Some have estimated that approaching one hundred percent of British colonists who lived a reasonable distance from the Atlantic seaboard from New England to Georgia had an opportunity to hear Whitefield preach sometime between 1739 and the evangelist's death in 1770.

His hearers received a resonant, consistent message on every occasion. It was the message of the new birth of salvation. Religion would not save you, he said, nor would godly parents or mere moral observance. 'If we are not inwardly wrought upon, and changed by the powerful operations of the Holy Spirit,' he insisted, then we had no hope for salvation. Only the imputed 'righteousness of JESUS CHRIST' could give anyone that sure hope. You must be born again, Whitefield repeated over and over, in the tens of thousands of sermons he gave in his career. 'Nothing short of a thorough, sound conversion will avail for the salvation of thy soul.'

1. George Whitefield — the Anglican Evangelist
by Lee Gatiss

December 2014 saw the 300th birthday of the great English evangelist, George Whitefield.[1] Whitefield is remembered as a great evangelical. By those who (somewhat mistakenly) consider evangelical religion to have begun only in the 1730s, he is hailed as a founding father of evangelicalism.[2]

His name has been honoured and kept alive in recent years by evangelical Baptists and Presbyterians, but he has been strangely undervalued by those in the Church of England itself. Furthermore, his identity as an Anglican has, therefore, been somewhat obscured.

1.1. *Positively Anglican*

Yet Whitefield himself would have identified his churchmanship as classically, positively, 'Anglican.' As Jim Packer puts it, 'like all England's evangelical clergy then and since, Whitefield insisted that the religion he modelled and taught was a straightforward application of Anglican doctrine as defined in the Articles, the Homilies and the Prayer Book.'[3] Or as Arnold Dallimore put it, 'He preached nothing but the basic doctrines of the Church of England; in glowing contrast to the majority of the clergy.'[4]

---

[1] A modified version of this chapter first appeared in *The Southern Baptist Journal of Theology* 18/2 (Summer 2014), pp 71-81, an issue devoted entirely to Whitefield, his impact and influence.

[2] I refer of course to David Bebbington's classic statement of this thesis in *Evangelicalism in Modern Britain: A History from the 1730s to the 1980s* (London: Routledge, 1989). See the devastating reassessment of this position by a wide variety of scholars in M.A.G. Haykin and K.J. Stewart (eds.), *The Emergence of Evangelicalism: Exploring historical continuities* (Nottingham: Apollos, 2008).

[3] J.I. Packer, 'The Spirit with the Word: The Reformational Revivalism of George Whitefield' in *Honouring the People of God: The Collected Shorter Writings of J.I. Packer* Volume 4 (Carlisle: Paternoster, 1999), p 51.

[4] Arnold Dallimore, *George Whitefield: The Life and Times of the Great evangelist of the 18th Century Revival*. Volume 1 (Edinburgh: Banner of Truth, 1970), p 116. On the last point, that the clergy themselves had abandoned the Church's true doctrine, a classic exposition of this was Jonathan Warne's *The Church of England Turned Dissenter* (1740), a book which carried a printed endorsement from Whitefield.

Reading through Whitefield's works we can easily observe this confessional slant to his ministry. Here we find quotations from the *Thirty-nine Articles of Religion*, especially where they touch on the doctrines of justification, predestination, original sin, and the place of good works. There are also many allusions to liturgical texts from the *Book of Common Prayer*, which Whitefield considered to embody the theology of the Articles and indeed of the Bible itself. It was 'one of the most excellent forms of public prayer in the world,' he said.[5] What was his view of the Church of England? 'My dear brethren, I am a friend to her Articles, I am a friend to her Homilies, I am a friend to her liturgy. And, if they did not thrust me out of their churches, I would read them every day.'[6]

The 'Homilies' he mentions were set sermons that had been first published under Edward VI in 1547, for use by clergy who were unable or unlicensed to compose their own. They are referred to in the Articles as containing 'godly and wholesome doctrine', and set forth, for the most part, Reformed and Evangelical truths about scripture, salvation, sin, and the sacraments. He planned a cheap edition of a selection of the Homilies, with a hymn and a prayer to accompany each one. He said in the preface he composed for that new edition (which sadly never materialised, as far as I am aware), that if these Homilies were preached more often, those like him who were deemed enthusiasts, madmen, troublers of Israel, and preachers of strange doctrine would be recognised, rather, as steady adherents to the wholesome doctrine of the Church of England. He lamented that they were so poorly known because so seldom reprinted, distributed, or read (by contrast to the Westminster Standards in Scotland, which were 'almost in every hand; and so constantly explained and insisted on').[7]

To that end, in the orphan house and school he set up in Georgia, he insisted that not only were the children to learn and repeat the

---

[5] Arnold Dallimore, *George Whitefield: The Life and Times of the Great Evangelist of the 18th Century Revival.* Volume 2 (Edinburgh: Banner of Truth, 1980), p. 470.

[6] Lee Gatiss (ed.), *The Sermons of George Whitefield.* Volume 1 (Wheaton, IL.: Crossway, 2012), p 176.

[7] See *The Works of the Reverend. George Whitefield:* Volume IV (London, 1771), pp 441-444. The Homilies can be found in John Griffiths (ed.), *The Two Books of Homilies* (Oxford: Oxford University Press, 1859), and there is a good critical edition of the first book, and an informative introduction, in Ronald Bond (ed.), *Certain Sermons or Homilies (1547) and A Homily against Disobedience and Wilful Rebellion (1570): A Critical Edition* (London: University of Toronto Press, 1987).

Thirty-nine Articles, but that the Homilies were to be well known too. 'The homilies to be read publicly, distinctly, frequently and carefully, every year, by the students, deputed in rotation', he specified.[8] Their education was to be a confessional education, he insisted. Whitefield also insisted on understanding the formularies of the Church in their plain grammatical sense. He had no time for the ambiguous doublespeak of Arminian and other commentators on the *Thirty-nine Articles*, for example. The original authors of the Anglican confession would not thank men whose 'two-fold interpretation' of the Articles 'opened a door for the most detestable equivocation.'[9]

1.2. The Anglican Doctrine of the Indwelling Spirit

Whitefield often glances at the Articles and Prayer Book in his sermons. Let us examine one sermon in particular to sample his method — his sermon on John 7:37-39, 'The Indwelling of the Spirit, the Common Privilege of All Believers.'[10]

This was preached in Bexley, in Kent. We know from his journal that during 1739 Whitefield had preached there. On one occasion, he had been expected to preach, but the local bishop demanded that the vicar deny him the use of the pulpit. So it was a tense period of resistance to his ministry. As he wrote at that time, 'If we have done anything worthy of the censures of the church, why do not the Right Reverend Bishops call us to a public account? If not, why do not they confess and own us?'[11]

So Whitefield was keen, in this atmosphere, to demonstrate that what he was preaching was fully in accord with the official doctrine of the Church of England. This sermon on the Holy Spirit, thought to be a distinctively evangelical doctrine, was a perfect place to demonstrate that harmony. Whitefield once said that 'the grand controversy God has with

---

[8] *The Works of the Reverend George Whitefield:* Volume III (London, 1771), p 499.
[9] *George Whitefield's Journals* (Edinburgh: Banner of Truth, 1960), p 429. He is referring primarily to Bishop Gilbert Burnet, whose infamous 1699 exposition of the *Thirty-nine Articles* alleged that they were susceptible to both Reformed and Arminian readings at key points. On Burnet's commentary, and the controversy surrounding it, see Stephen Hampton, *Anti-Arminians: The Anglican Reformed Tradition from Charles II to George I* (Oxford: Oxford University Press, 2008), pp 28-31.
[10] Lee Gatiss (ed.), *The Sermons of George Whitefield*. Volume 2 (Wheaton, IL.: Crossway, 2012), pp 115-128.
[11] *George Whitefield's Journals*, p 293.

England is for the slight put on the Holy Ghost. As soon as a person begins to talk of the work of the Holy Ghost, they cry, "you are a Methodist": as soon as you speak about the divine influences of the Holy Ghost, "O!" say they, "you are an enthusiast."'[12]

So he begins his sermon on this text by pointing out that those who talk about receiving God's Spirit 'are looked upon by some as enthusiasts and madmen. And by others represented as wilfully deceiving the people and undermining the established constitution of the church.'[13] Yet when Jesus spoke of flowing rivers of living water and John explained that this was about the Spirit, 'which they that believe on him shall receive,' he was not talking simply about the first apostles, but about all subsequent believers. As a text for Trinity Sunday in the Anglican church calendar, John 7 was apt to demonstrate that the Trinity was not a complex doctrine designed to confuse us, but a delight and comfort to all the faithful.

Whitefield alludes to the set prayer for the day, the proper preface for Trinity Sunday, and makes it clear that he understands the person of the Spirit to be 'consubstantial and co-eternal with the Father and the Son, proceeding from, yet equal to them both.' This is entirely in accord with the Athanasian Creed, appointed to be said or sung that day at Morning Prayer, and with Article 5. The 'excellent' Communion Service in the *Book of Common Prayer* says of those who receive the sacrament rightly that they 'dwell in Christ and Christ in them; that they are one with Christ and Christ with them.' So, says Whitefield, 'every Christian, in the proper sense of the word, must be an enthusiast' and united to God by receiving the Holy Ghost.[14]

'Letter-learned preachers' deny this doctrine in reality, he claims. Yet, he says, 'I am astonished that any who call themselves members, much more, that many who are preachers in the Church of England, should dare so much as to open their lips against it.' It is impossible to approve the liturgy of the Church 'and yet deny the Holy Spirit to be the portion of all believers.' He goes on to quote various parts of the authorised liturgy which make reference to the Spirit and his indwelling.

---

[12] *Eighteen Sermons Preached by the Late Rev. George Whitefield A.M.* (London, 1771), pp 381-382.
[13] Gatiss (ed.), *Sermons*, Vol. 2, p 115.
[14] Gatiss (ed.), *Sermons*, Vol. 2, pp 117, 119.

For example, the daily absolution asks God to grant his Spirit to the repentant. The collect or set prayer for Christmas Day asks God to 'daily renew us by his Holy Spirit.' And in the collect for the day of Pentecost, or Whitsunday, we pray to 'rejoice in the comforts of the Holy Ghost.' Both the baptismal formula of Matthew 28 (used in the christening service) and 'the grace' of 2 Corinthians 13 (used at the end of Evening Prayer) are explicitly Trinitarian, and show that the Spirit is with us, as we are baptised into his name and his fellowship.[15]

Whitefield goes on to make the denial of the indwelling of the Spirit even more uncomfortable for ministers. Quoting the Ordinal, the set services in which they were ordained, he reminds every clergyman that 'they trust they are inwardly moved by the Holy Ghost, to take upon them that administration.' As a man is ordained presbyter, the bishop is to say, 'Receive the Holy Ghost... now committed unto thee, by the imposition of our hands.' How then can those who insist on the necessity of receiving the Holy Spirit be called 'madmen, enthusiasts, schismatics, and underminers of the established constitution'? It is not true of all, but 'the generality of the clergy are fallen from our Articles and do not speak agreeable to them, or to the form of sound words delivered in the Scriptures', he said. For their hypocrisy — 'How can they escape the damnation of hell?'[16]

Later in this same sermon he quotes from Article 9 to establish the doctrine of original sin. But his main use of the formularies has been to demonstrate quite decisively that evangelical doctrine is Anglican doctrine. The conclusion for Whitefield seemed to be that if this is truly so, he should be left unmolested by the authorities to preach and proclaim this doctrine wherever and whenever he saw fit. That may not logically follow, perhaps. There is a case for good order and obedience to it. But he was certainly correct when he concluded that: 'Would we restore the church to its primitive dignity, the only way is to live and preach the doctrine of Christ and the Articles to which we have subscribed. Then we shall find the number of dissenters will daily decrease and the church of England become the joy of the whole earth.'[17]

---

[15] Gatiss (ed.), *Sermons*, Vol. 2, p 120.
[16] Gatiss (ed.), *Sermons*, Vol. 2, p 121. See also his letter in *Works*, Vol. IV, p 300, where he also quotes the set hymn for ordinations, 'Come, Holy Ghost, our souls inspire'.
[17] Gatiss (ed.), *Sermons*, Vol. 2, p 122.

Whitefield, therefore, was unashamedly a confessional evangelical. He was delighted not only to prove his evangelical doctrines from the scriptures, but to find them in the confessional documents of the national church, expound them from there, and call those who had subscribed to such standards to preach and live by the same. For him the *Thirty-nine Articles* and the *Book of Common Prayer* were not dusty relics of a forgotten past. If deployed well, they pointed people to the evangelical gospel, the way of salvation, and the path of life as well as being useful for refuting those who would lead us astray.

1.3. Anglican Cavalryman

Whitefield's paternal grandfather, Andrew Whitefield, had been a successful businessman in Bristol which enabled him to retire early and live the life of a country gentleman. His father too was a businessman and George inherited a certain entrepreneurial streak from these men which made him go looking for opportunities to expand his ministry. Far from taking early retirement, however, he worked himself into an early grave, and died in his mid-50s!

Upon his first return to England from Georgia, George Whitefield found that many pulpits were closed to his fundraising work for the orphanage he supported there, due to his youthful over-exuberance in denouncing the clergy in his early sermons. He took this opportunity to begin a new phase of evangelical mission in this country. His first step out of the established mould had been to go to Georgia, a brand new colony in America designed to take the poor and criminal elements from England and put them to good use (much as would happen in Australia some time later). Never becoming the incumbent of an ordinary parish, Whitefield was one of those who thrived on the edges of the establishment, and so when itinerant preaching proved more difficult in churches he took to the open air and began to preach anywhere and everywhere he could.

Rather than waiting for people to invite him to preach or hoping that sinners would come to hear, he adopted the more aggressive strategy of going out and calling to them, in the 'highways and byways,' rejoicing that this tactic had Gospel precedent and dominical sanction (Luke 14:23). 'The world is now my parish' he had declared six weeks after being ordained (antedating Wesley's now more famous use of this phrase by a month).[18] The grey skies of London, Bristol, and other cities became like the dome of his very own cathedral into which thousands of people poured to hear this curious and dramatic Anglican clergyman.

Augustus Toplady narrates how his hero Whitefield once tried to persuade him to become an itinerant preacher too, encouraging the younger man with promises of greater fruitfulness should he do so. Yet as Toplady told Lady Huntingdon, 'I consider the true ministers of God as providentially divided into two bands: viz., the regulars and the irregulars.' Some such as Whitefield were akin to cavalry and others, like him, were more like sentinels or guardsmen watching over a more circumscribed district.[19]

Toplady could see the great blessing that the irregular and unusual ministry of men like Whitefield had been, but did not think it was for him, or for everyone; an ordinary Reformed Evangelical parochial ministry within the Church of England structures was just as vital and important as the more high-profile 'celebrity' roles.

Yet Whitefield was clearly in his element as an Anglican cavalryman, with a self-endangering and self-sacrificing boldness which earned him the respect of many of his contemporaries. The important thing to notice is that other evangelicals in the Church of England like Toplady, William Romaine, and James Hervey – the regular guardsmen – considered Whitefield no less Anglican for his more irregular tactics. He always remained doctrinally in line with the Anglican heritage even when he was being more adventurous in terms of institutional order. He was not only evangelistically enterprising but also positively Anglican.

Yet even cavalry need to have a settled base camp from which to operate. Eventually this led to Whitefield planting three churches: 'The Tabernacle' in East London at Moorfields, a chapel on Tottenham Court Road in the West End, and another 'Tabernacle' in Bristol. Add to this the orphanage in Georgia and a school at Kingswood and it is clear that Whitefield had a flair for fundraising and starting new projects, as platforms for gospel ministry. He had great entrepreneurial spirit.

His expertise did not, however, extend to the maintenance of 'empire.' In that department he was far outstripped by the imperious

---

[18] See Boyd Stanley Schlenther, 'Whitefield, George (1714–1770)' in *Oxford Dictionary of National Biography* (Oxford: Oxford University Press, 2004).

[19] A. M. Toplady, *The Complete Works of Augustus Toplady* (Harrisonburg, Virginia: Sprinkle Publications, 1987), p 862.

John Wesley. He lost the school to Wesley, and the orphanage did not develop as he hoped, being saddled with a huge debt by the time that Whitefield died. Yet it is clear that with his entrepreneurial and radical style of Anglicanism, Toplady was not saying too much when he styled Whitefield, 'The apostle of the English empire' as well as 'a true and faithful son of the Church of England.'[20]

Whitefield sought to extend the boundaries of the Church into places where no church buildings had yet been put up, where the ordinary parochial ministry had failed or had not even attempted to reach the populace. He found the harvest was plentiful though the workers were few (Matthew 9:37-38) and obeyed his ordination call (as the *Ordinal* annexed to the *Book of Common Prayer* puts it), 'to seek for Christ's sheep that are dispersed abroad, and for his children who are in the midst of this naughty world, that they may be saved through Christ for ever... For they are the sheep of Christ, which he bought with his death, and for whom he shed his blood.'

1.4. Facing opposition from Anglican authorities

Whitefield faced a great deal of opposition from within the Church of England. Naturally, that in itself does not mean that one is not an Anglican, necessarily. What is it that Whitefield was criticised and censured for?

Certainly he was criticised for his doctrine. And we have just seen how he defended himself from such attacks by utilising the official formularies of the Church. However, in his journals he also records a number of occasions where the issue, in essence, was one not of doctrine but of order. That is, he was called to account for not observing the niceties of decorum and the parish system.

About a month after he was ordained a presbyter at Christ Church, Oxford, Whitefield was summoned by the Chancellor of Bristol Diocese. He had preached in various churches in the diocese, raising support for his orphanage in Georgia. He had also been preaching in the prison, and to the poor miners in Kingswood. But the Chancellor was not happy that he did so without a specific license from the bishop of that diocese. The Chancellor appealed to various obsolete canons of the Church,

---

[20] 'A Concise Character of the Late Rev. Mr. Whitefield' in Toplady, *The Complete Works*, p 494.

which he had not enforced on other visiting preachers. Whitefield responded by asking why other canons, such as those which forbade clergy from frequenting taverns and playing cards, were not also enforced on others. The Chancellor accused him of preaching false doctrine, but later confessed to never having heard him preach or read his writings.[21]

A few months later, he heard that a friend was considering leaving the Church of England (denying Christ's visible church on earth, as he put it). Whitefield pleaded with him not to secede, saying 'consider, my dear brother, what confusion your separation from the church will occasion.' Whitefield found being an Anglican a great help to evangelism, he said: 'I can assure you that my being a minister of the Church of England, and preaching its Articles, is a means under God of drawing so many after me.' As for objecting to the robes that clergy were meant to wear, about which this friend had expressed scruples, 'Good God!' he exclaimed, 'I thought we long since knew that the kingdom of God did not consist in any externals, but in righteousness and peace and joy in the Holy Spirit.'[22]

Two days after writing this letter urging his friend to remain an Anglican, the Chancellor of Bristol was chasing after Whitefield again, and angrily threatening him (and those who met to hear him) with imprisonment. Yet he was never persuaded even by this to become a nonconformist. 'For my own part,' he said, 'I can see no reason for my leaving the Church, however I am treated by the corrupt members and ministers of it. I judge of the state of a Church, not from the practice of its members, but its primitive and public constitutions; and so long as I think the Articles of the Church of England are agreeable to Scripture, I am resolved to preach them up without either bigotry or party zeal. For I love all who love the Lord Jesus.'[23]

Whitefield was pursued by the authorities for irregularity, that is, preaching outside and away from a settled parish ministry.[24] But in some ways he courted this opposition, in a most unhelpful way. In July 1739 he records how he went to St Paul's Cathedral one day to take the Lord's Supper, as a testimony that he was a law-abiding Anglican. Then

---

[21] *George Whitefield's Journals*, pp 218-219, 221.
[22] *George Whitefield's Journals*, pp 255-256.
[23] *George Whitefield's Journals*, p 256.
[24] See his letter to the Bishop of Gloucester on the subject in *Works*, Vol. IV, p 17.

he went straight to preach on Kennington Common, to about 30,000 people he says. And what did he preach?

> God gave me great power, and I never opened my mouth so freely against the letter-learned clergymen of the Church of England. Every day do I see the necessity of speaking out more and more. God knows my heart, I do not speak out of resentment. I heartily wish all the Lord's servants were prophets; I wish the Church of England was the joy of the whole earth; but I cannot see her sinking into papistical ignorance, and refined deism, and not open my mouth against those who, by their sensual, lukewarm lives, and unscriptural superficial doctrines, thus cause her to err.[25]

No doubt it is right to oppose papistical ignorance and refined deism, yet one must not be surprised if 'letter-learned clergyman' are not exactly ecstatic about being denounced in public by a twenty-four year old itinerant. Others too may be just a little suspicious that the young man's motives were less spiritual than he professed. It could appear to many that he was simply looking to make a name for himself.

Some dissenters, those nonconformists outside the Church of England, were quite wary about Whitefield. In 1743, after Whitefield preached in Phillip Doddridge's church in Northampton, Doddridge was rebuked by his fellow dissenters. Nathaniel Neal wrote to him expressing 'utmost concern' that he was associating with someone accused of 'imprudencies' and 'a forward and indiscreet zeal, and an unsettled injudicious way of thinking and behaving'.[26] David Jennings told him that he should sever all his ties with Whitefield.[27] Doddridge admitted himself that Whitefield was 'a very honest tho a very weak Man. ... He certainly does much good & I am afraid some harm.'[28] He praised Whitefield's oratory, but was careful to add that he was 'not so zealously attached to him as to be disposed to celebrate him as one of the greatest men of the age, or to think that he is the pillar that bears up

---

[25] *George Whitefield's Journals*, p 312.
[26] Nathaniel Neal to Philip Doddridge, 11 October 1743, Humphreys, *Correspondence*, Vol. 4, pp 274-75 (Nuttall, *Calendar*, Letter no. 922). I am very grateful to Robert Strivens for the references to Whitefield in the Doddridge correspondence, which he includes in his PhD.
[27] David Jennings to Philip Doddridge, 20 October 1743, DWL MS 71.15 (Nuttall, *Additional Letters*, Letter no. 924A).
[28] Philip Doddridge to Daniel Wadsworth, n. d.., DWL, Congregational Library Reed MSS 34 (Nuttall, *Calendar*, Letter no. 705).

the whole interest of religion among us'.[29] Doddridge kept some distance between himself and the great Anglican evangelist, because proper order and a sober judgment about celebrities was important to him, as it is for many today.

1.5. An Anglican Evangelical Criticism of Whitefield

Whitefield may be fairly criticised, despite his love for the Church of England, for actually undermining it in one respect. As Jim Packer insightfully puts it, he 'did in fact unwittingly encourage an individualistic piety of what we would call a parachurch type, a piety that gave its prime loyalty to transdenominational endeavours, that became impatient and restless in face of the relatively fixed forms of institutional church life, and that conceived of evangelism as typically an extra-ecclesiastical activity.'[30]

He may not have wished to have this effect, but he did. People flocked to hear the celebrity, and began to think that all established local churches must be, as Mr Whitefield said, dead and lifeless. So they became attached to his more free-floating type of ministry, less rooted in the deep structures of communities and churches. They began to think that effective evangelism could only be done outside the church, in large public meetings.

It has taken evangelicals in the Church of England, and elsewhere, many years to rediscover the local church itself as a vehicle for evangelism. We must continue to value this God-given means for reaching our nation for Christ and not rely entirely on extra-parochial, parachurch missionary activity. A passion to see new spiritual life through evangelism must, rather, be part of the DNA of each local church, whatever is happening elsewhere. They should not leave it to 'the professionals' because they feel inadequate, or out of ignorance and

---

[29] Nathaniel Neal to Philip Doddridge, 10 December 1743, Humphreys, *Correspondence*, Vol. 4, p 288 (Nuttall, *Calendar*, Letter no. 933). Philip Doddridge to Nathaniel Neal, 12 December 1743, Humphreys, *Correspondence*, Vol. 4, p 292 (Nuttall, *Calendar*, Letter no. 934).

[30] Packer, 'Reformational Revivalism', p 59. L. B. Schenck, *The Presbyterian Doctrine of Children in the Covenant: A Historical Study of the Significance of Infant Baptism in the Presbyterian Church* (Phillipsburg, NJ.: P&R, 2003), also criticises preachers of the Great Awakening (including Whitefield) for weakening people's belief in the doctrines of infant baptism and covenantal inclusion by their insistence on dramatic (or at least conscious) experiences of new birth.

fear.[31] Parachurch agencies (such as the one that I currently serve) must constantly remind people that they are not the church, but are here to serve the church, the true arena of the gospel.

A church which is simultaneously a 'shop front' for outsiders, a nursery for new Christians, and a family in which to serve and grow is a magnificent blessing for any community, no matter how large it happens to be. It was designed by God to be so. Our networks and coalitions and partnerships and seminaries and societies exist to serve such churches. It is not meant to be the other way around, so that parachurch ministries and their celebrity leaders are exalted at the expense of the true heroes on the front line.

That being said, Whitefield's 'storm trooper' activity gave huge impetus to the evangelical party within the Church of England. He was also keen to foster relations with those outside the pale of the established church, being a man with a famously 'catholic spirit.'[32] He says in one sermon that, 'There is nothing grieves me more than the differences amongst God's people,'[33] and he sought to work with any who loved the Lord in sincerity and truth, even if that meant a loss of face for him.

He was able to work, despite some massive theological differences, even with John Wesley on occasion, yet only by renouncing all his leadership roles in England and Wales in 1748 and appearing merely as one of Wesley's 'assistants.' Wesley's ego couldn't allow him an equal place on the platform, but Whitefield did not complain. This speaks volumes about the true interests of both men, perhaps, but certainly about the humility of Whitefield and his willingness to work with those outside his own theological comfort zones. Unlike Wesley, he was also able to work with nonconformists, whom Wesley often despised and avoided.

This, however, was a function of Whitefield's other distinctive, his Reformed theology, and of Wesley's more sectarian Arminianism, not to mention his upbringing.[34] Whitefield castigated Wesley for saying

---

[31] See Mark Dever, *Nine Marks of a Healthy Church* (Wheaton, IL.: Crossway, 2000), p 106.
[32] See the inspiring, 'George Whitefield and Christian Unity' in Iain Murray's, *Heroes* (Edinburgh: Banner of Truth, 2008), pp 47-83.
[33] Gatiss (ed.), *Sermons*, Vol. 1, p 400.
[34] According to I. Murray, *Wesley and Men Who Followed* (Edinburgh: Banner of Truth, 2003), pp 12-16, Wesley's father was once arrested and imprisoned for speaking so furiously against dissenters.

that no Baptist or Presbyterian writer knew anything of the liberties of Christ.[35] It is however vital to remember that Whitefield considered the Church of England itself to be 'Reformed', even 'Calvinist', and was in no way unusual for holding to that view. It had been held by archbishops, bishops, clergy, theologians, and laypeople before him, many of whom he quotes with approval in his sermons (such as bishops Hall and Beveridge and archbishop Ussher). He was conscious of standing in a noble line of theological predecessors, part of a venerable and distinguished tradition.[36]

1.6. Conclusion

George Whitefield was a mighty man of God, greatly used for the furtherance of the gospel on both sides of the Atlantic. We rejoice in his evangelical faith, but let us also be aware of and remember his Anglican convictions. From life's first cry to final breath, he was a confessional Church of England man. It wasn't always easy — he needed some guts and some resilience to stick it out under pressure. He knew they weren't perfect, but he loved the Articles, the Homilies, the Liturgy, and he used them for the gospel, to win people for Christ, and to build the evangelical cause in the church of his day.

So then, Anglican brothers and sisters, let us go and do likewise. And may we all, whether cavalry or infantry, be enthusiastically, entrepreneurially evangelical, as was the great Anglican Evangelist, George Whitefield.

1.7. Sources

Bebbington, David. *Evangelicalism in Modern Britain: A History from the 1730s to the 1980s*. London: Routledge, 1989.

Bond (ed.), Ronald. *Certain Sermons or Homilies (1547) and A Homily against Disobedience and Wilful Rebellion (1570): A Critical Edition*. London: University of Toronto Press, 1987.

Dallimore, Arnold. *George Whitefield: The Life and Times of the Great evangelist of the 18th Century Revival*. Volume 1. Edinburgh: Banner of Truth, 1970.

_____. *George Whitefield: The Life and Times of the Great Evangelist of the 18th Century Revival*. Volume 2. Edinburgh: Banner of Truth, 1980.

---

[35] See *George Whitefield's Journals*, pp 583.
[36] For more on this see Lee Gatiss, *The True Profession of the Gospel: Augustus Toplady and Reclaiming our Reformed Foundations* (London: Latimer Trust, 2010), pp 29-51.

Dever, Mark. *Nine Marks of a Healthy Church*. Wheaton, IL.: Crossway, 2000.
Gatiss (ed.), Lee. *The Sermons of George Whitefield*. Volume 1. Wheaton, IL.: Crossway, 2012.
_____. *The Sermons of George Whitefield*. Volume 2. Wheaton, IL.: Crossway, 2012.
_____. *The True Profession of the Gospel: Augustus Toplady and Reclaiming our Reformed Foundations*. London: Latimer Trust, 2010.
Griffiths (ed.), John. *The Two Books of Homilies*. Oxford: Oxford University Press, 1859.
Hampton, Stephen. *Anti-Arminians: The Anglican Reformed Tradition from Charles II to George I*. Oxford: Oxford University Press, 2008.
Haykin, M.A.G. and Stewart (eds.), K.J. *The Emergence of Evangelicalism: Exploring historical continuities*. Nottingham: Apollos, 2008.
Murray's, Ian. *Heroes*. Edinburgh: Banner of Truth, 2008.
_____. *Wesley and Men Who Followed*. Edinburgh: Banner of Truth, 2003.
Nuttall, G.F. *Calendar of the correspondence of Philip Doddridge, DD, (1702-1751)*, Letter nos. 705, 922, 933, 934
_____. *Additional Letters*, Letter no. 924A
Packer, J.I. 'The Spirit with the Word: The Reformational Revivalism of George Whitefield' in *Honouring the People of God: The Collected Shorter Writings of J.I. Packer* Volume 4. Carlisle: Paternoster, 1999.
Schenck, L.B. *The Presbyterian Doctrine of Children in the Covenant: A Historical Study of the Significance of Infant Baptism in the Presbyterian Church*. Phillipsburg, NJ.: P&R, 2003.
Schlenther, Boyd Stanley. 'Whitefield, George (1714–1770)' *Oxford Dictionary of National Biography*. Oxford: Oxford University Press, 2004.
Toplady, A. M. *The Complete Works of Augustus Toplady*. Harrisonburg, Virginia: Sprinkle Publications, 1987.
Warne, Jonathan. *The Church of England Turned Dissenter*. London: T. Cooper, 1737.
Whitefield, George. *The Works of the Reverend George Whitefield: Volume III, IV*. London, 1771.
_____. *George Whitefield's Journals*, Edinburgh: Banner of Truth, 1960.
_____. *Eighteen Sermons Preached by the Late Rev. George Whitefield A.M.* London, 1771.

2. George Whitefield and Preached Calvinism
by Melvin Tinker

2.1. Introduction

It is the commonly received view that Calvinism is incompatible with authentic evangelism, that its central tenets cut the throat of all vigorous evangelistic endeavours.[1]

But the towering figure of George Whitefield in the 18th Century should be sufficient to silence such a view once and for all. Whitefield did not have to engage in 'double think' – putting his Calvinist principles to one side while he got on with the practical task of evangelism; indeed, as we shall see, Whitefield's deep doctrinal convictions provided the oxygen which enabled his evangelism to burn with such white hot intensity.

That George Whitefield was a Calvinist is not in doubt: 'From first to last,' Professor Harry Stout says, 'he was a Calvinist who believed that God chose him for salvation and not the reverse.'[2] Writing on February 20, 1741, to Anne Dutton, Whitefield refers to his settlement in Georgia and says, 'My family in Georgia was once sadly shaken, but now, blessed be God, it is settled, and, I hope, established in the doctrines of grace.'[3] Whitefield's own claim was that his Calvinism was not 'second hand', having been derived from a reading of John Calvin, but from his own reading of Scripture with the aid of Matthew Henry.[4] 'I embrace the Calvinistic scheme,' he said, 'not because Calvin, but Jesus Christ has taught it to me.'[5] Elsewhere he asserted, 'I am a staunch Calvinist.'[6] 'I profess myself a Calvinist as to principle.'[7]

---

[1] See Roger E. Olson, *Against Calvinism* (Grand Rapids, MI: Zondervan, 2011); ch 6.
[2] Harry S. Stout, *The Divine Dramatist: George Whitefield and the Rise of Modern Evangelicalism* (Grand Rapids, MI: Eerdmans, 1991), p xxxiii.
[3] Michael A. G. Haykin, *The Revived Puritan: The Spirituality of George Whitefield* (Dundas, Ontario: Joshua Press, 2000), p 127.
[4] Haykin, *The Revived Puritan*, p 26.
[5] *The Letters of George Whitefield, 1734-42* (Edinburgh: Banner of Truth, 1976), p 442.
[6] George Whitefield, 'Additional Letters' (Letter 29, May 21st, 1746), *The Works of George Whitefield* (Oswestry: Quinta Press, 2000), p 39.
[7] George Whitefield, 'Additional Sermons' (Sermon LXII), *The Works of George Whitefield* (Oswestry: Quinta Press, 2000), p 71.

While there may be little to dispute concerning the applicability of the term 'Calvinist' to George Whitefield[8], a number of questions are raised which centre upon Whitefield's Calvinistic beliefs: What was the nature of Whitefield's Calvinism? When did such beliefs begin to be embraced and how genuine were they? How did Whitefield's Calvinism find expression, especially in his preaching, which by any standards was formidable? These are some of the questions this paper seeks to explore together with a brief consideration of the relevance of Whitefield's convictions for Gospel ministry today.

2.2. Which Calvinism?

The term 'Calvinism' was first used by Lutheran theologians to refer to what they regarded as the peculiar views of Christ's real presence at the Lord's Supper held by John Calvin and his followers. Since then, the term has taken on significantly different meanings. In some instances it denotes the entire theological system of Calvin as found in the four books of his *Institutes*. More commonly it refers to the understanding of the doctrine of salvation as found in the first three books. There is a difference between the two in that the fourth book, which many consider to be the climax of his thinking, develops his views of ecclesiology and the relation between church and state.[9] In terms of church government, this is decidedly Presbyterian, and in relation to the state, the magistrate is considered to be God's minister. Clearly, Whitefield, being an ordained minister in the Church of England was not the former, but in terms of his beliefs regarding the nature and means of salvation he certainly was the latter. In short he was a 'doctrinal' Calvinist.

Here we come to the heart of the Calvinist system, which was captured by the terms used by Whitefield to which we have already referred, namely, 'the doctrines of grace'. The rallying cry is 'salvation by grace alone.' As we shall see by reference to his preaching, Whitefield

---

[8] 'It is no accident that both George Whitefield and Howell Harris chose to deliberately define themselves as Calvinists. They were proud of the fact that they stood within a Calvinist tradition that, in Harris's words, "stretched back to the good old Reformers and Puritans."' David C. Jones, Eryn M. White and Boyd S. Schlenther, *The Elect Methodists: Calvinistic Methodism in England and Wales, 1735-1811*, (Cardiff: The University of Wales Press, 2012), p 2.

[9] See Paul Helm, 'The Many Shades of Calvinism', http://paulhelmsdeep.blogspot.com/2011/03/many-shades-of-calvinism.html [accessed 12.08.2015].

followed Calvin 'from a distance' as it were, in so far as Calvin followed Augustine who in turn followed the teaching of the apostle Paul. This was clearly recognised by his one-time friend and theological opponent John Wesley, who, in his memorial sermon for Whitefield declared, 'His fundamental point was, "Give God all the glory of whatever is good in man;" and "In the business of salvation, set Christ as high and man as low as possible."' With this point he and his friends at Oxford, the original Methodists, so called, set out. Their grand principle was: 'There is no power (by nature) and no merit in man. They insisted, all power to think, speak or act aright, is in and from the Spirit of Christ.'[10]

Paul Helm asks if there is a test for whether someone understands and accepts the gospel of grace understood in this Pauline, Augustinian, Calvinistic sense. He doubts that a 'fool-proof' test exists, but nonetheless puts forward the following as a reliable guide:

> In his wonderful letter to the Romans Paul reaches the peak of his exposition of God's grace in Jesus Christ in Romans 8. Before that (in, roughly, Chapters 3-5) he expounded our salvation as founded on God's justification of the ungodly (Romans 4:5). This is inseparably connected with our sanctification, a new life of union with Christ as we are buried with him in his baptism and raised with him in newness of life (Ch. 6). It is characterised by a never-ending struggle between the old sinful nature (the 'flesh' as Paul puts it) and the 'new man' (the spirit) (Ch. 7). The Romans 8 climax is like a chain (the 'golden chaine', as earlier Reformed types called it).[11] Beginning in Romans 8:29 with God's eternal purpose, *For those whom he foreknew* (his knowledge of whom he will save), *he also predestined to be conformed to the image of his Son* (his actual destining of his chosen ones to be conformed to the image of his Son Jesus Christ). Paul goes on, *And those whom he predestined he also called* (effectually called ...) *and those whom he called he also justified* (pardoned and reckoned righteous in Christ); *and those whom he justified those he also glorified ... What shall we say to these things? If God is for us, who can be against us?* (ESV). From first (foreknowing) to last (glorifying) Paul says that the work is God's work, and the

---

[10] Thomas Jackson (ed.), *The Works of John Wesley*. Vol. 6. (Grand Rapids, MI: Baker Book House, 1986), p 178.
[11] Whitefield himself refers to the 'golden chain' in relation to the doctrine of perseverance in his sermon, 'Christ the Believer's Wisdom, Righteousness, Sanctification, and Redemption,' in Lee Gatiss (ed.), *The Sermons of George Whitefield*. Vol. 2. (Wheaton, IL: Crossway, 2012), p 220.

chain from the first to the last is unbreakable, (note the 'also's'), holding the people of God steady and secure in God's grace from first to last. Is there a test of being 'Reformed' or being 'Calvinistic' in the muddled and confusing Christian world of [today]? I say that if we feel the need of one, there is. It's the unqualified recognition of Paul's golden chain of Romans 8.[12]

If this guide is reliable, then we can say that Whitefield was a full-blooded doctrinal Calvinist of the first order.

As we have seen, the beliefs Whitefield held were not adopted because of a prior allegiance to the teachings of John Calvin *per se*, but because he believed that they were the plain teaching of Scripture itself. However, while Whitefield held to the Reformed principle of *sola Scriptura* he did not follow the leanings of some evangelicals today towards *sola exegesis*.[13] He valued the wisdom and the 'systematised' theology expressed within the articles of his own church. Here he found clear backing for his Calvinist beliefs, he writes, 'This is my comfort, the doctrines I have taught are the doctrines of Scripture, the doctrines of *our own* and of other reformed churches.'[14] Whitefield's certainty that he had the Thirty-Nine Articles of the Church of England on his side is also revealed in a letter he wrote against a sermon preached by John Wesley on free grace:

> Thirdly, in your sermon, on page 137 paragraph 12, "This doctrine tends to destroy the comforts of religion, the happiness of Christianity, &c." But how does Mr Wesley know this, who never believed in election? I believe they who have experienced it, will agree with our 17th article.[15]

---

[12] Helm, 'Shades of Calvinism'.

[13] 'What has happened is that modern Evangelicalism has been shaped by what can be best called a policy of *sola exegesis*, not *sola Scriptura* as the Reformers understood it ... Anyone who tries to preach the results of exegesis (as distilled, for example, in the average modern commentary) will soon discover one of two things. Either he will end up lecturing on the meaning of a particular verse or passage – an activity which may appeal to an intellectual minority but is unlikely to make a lasting impression on anyone's life – or he will abandon any serious attempt to apply the text and retreat to the old stand-by of experience, using the text as an introduction to what he really wants to say' (Gerald Bray, 'Whatever Happened to the Authority of Scripture?,' in Melvin Tinker (ed.), *The Anglican Evangelical Crisis* (Christian Focus Publications, 1995), pp 62-67.

[14] Letter CXV, *The Works of George Whitefield*. Vol. 1 (Oswestry: Quinta Press, 2000), p 129, and other similar statements from the same day; emphasis supplied.

[15] From Georgia, December 24th, 1740, *The Works of George Whitefield*. Vol. 4 (Oswestry: Quinta Press, 2000).

J. I. Packer is therefore quite correct to conclude that Whitefield was

> an Anglican Calvinist of the Puritan type. He embraced the sovereign-grace teaching of the Thirty-Nine Articles with regard to personal salvation (especially Articles 9-13 and 17), affirmed the developed federal theology of the seventeenth century, and insisted that sovereign-grace teaching, with its rejection of salvation by self-effort in all its forms, bears directly on the purity or otherwise of the believer's devotion.[16]

As Whitefield's sermons testify, his was no narrow, strict predestinarian form of Calvinism but one which, using today's theological terminology, could be described as *complementarian*[17] holding together in unsatisfied tension God's sovereignty and human responsibility, such that,

> [f]or Whitefield and the Calvinistic Methodists it was this embryonic tradition of evangelical Calvinism, with its twin emphases on conversion and heart nurture, which proved compelling. Indeed, in many respects, Whitefield was to be the most energetic champion of evangelical Calvinism in the eighteenth century, with the result that by the end of his life it had become the dominant expression of Reformed orthodoxy favoured by Calvinist-inclined evangelicals almost everywhere.[18]

2.3. An Authentic or Opportunistic Calvinist?

In 1876, Luke Tyerman put forward the theory that George Whitefield in the earliest years of his ministry was an Arminian.[19] Tyerman argued that he switched his position for purely pragmatic reasons, namely, to gain the patronage of the Countess of Huntingdon and more readily elicit the support of Dissenting ministers.

The view that Whitefield's thinking about Reformed soteriology was not settled until after 1739 has also been espoused by Arnold Dallimore, while nonetheless observing that as early as 1737 his outlook was

---

[16] J.I. Packer, 'The Reformational Revivalism of George Whitefield,' in *Honouring the People of God, The Collected Shorter Writings of J.I. Packer*. Vol. 2 (Carlisle: Paternoster, 1999), p 47.

[17] For a defence and exposition of this position, see Melvin Tinker, *Intended for Good: The Providence of God* (Nottingham: IVP, 2012), pp 31-43.

[18] Jones, White, and Schlenther, 'Elect Methodists', p 3.

[19] Luke Tyerman, *The Life of the Revd George Whitefield, B.A., of Pembroke College, Oxford*. Vol. I (London: Hodder and Stoughton, 1876), p 275.

moving in a decidedly Reformed direction, as evidenced by one of his earliest sermons which refers to justification, election, preservation of the saints, and particular or 'limited' atonement. Yet Dallimore is of the opinion that these did not constitute the core of Whitefield's teaching at this point, but acted as indicators that he was simply moving along a Reformed trajectory as, 'he was not fully clear in his own understanding of it.'[20] Whilst for Tyerman, Whitefield appears to be something of an opportunist, for Dallimore, he is a work in progress.

Jared Hood convincingly argues that both Tyerman and Dallimore have wrongly evaluated the evidence and misjudged Whitefield.[21] Hood argues that with the controversy with John Wesley becoming more intense and more public by mid-1739, Whitefield simply had to consider his ground on predestination more carefully than he had before.[22] In both his correspondence with John Wesley and Ralph Erskine, there is no indication that Whitefield believed that he had changed his position. Hood observes that, 'there may be a flurry of statements on the issue of election in 1739-1740, but one will not find the opposite kinds of statements in the pre-1739 period. The movement is from quiet expression to more dominant expression and that is all. There is no warrant for concluding that prior to 1739, Whitefield had not been preaching Calvinism.'[23] Indeed, in the quotation from Wesley's memorial sermon referenced above, it would seem clear that Wesley himself recognised Whitefield's Reformed principles from the very beginning of his Methodism at Oxford.

George Clarkson makes much of the oft quoted statement of Whitefield to John Wesley that he had 'never read Calvin', leading him to conclude, 'nor was he a follower of Calvin or John Knox as such.'[24] The alleged denial by Whitefield of reading Calvin appears in a letter to John Wesley dated August, 25th, 1740,

> I cannot bear the thoughts of opposing you: but how can I avoid it, if you go about (as your brother Charles once said) to drive *John Calvin* out of *Bristol.* Alas, I never read anything that *Calvin* wrote; my

---

[20] Arnold A. Dallimore, *George Whitefield: The Life and Times of the Great Evangelist of the 18th Century Revival.* Vol. 2 (Banner of Truth Trust, 1980), pp 25-26.
[21] Jared C. Hood, '"I never read Calvin"; George Whitefield, a Calvinist Untimely Born', *Churchman* 125/1 (2011), pp 7-20.
[22] Hood, 'I never read Calvin', p 10.
[23] Hood, 'I never read Calvin', p 11.
[24] George E. Clarkson, *George Whitefield and Welsh Calvinist Methodism* (Lampeter: Edwin Mellen Press, 1996), p 21.

doctrines I had from Christ and the apostles; I was taught them of GOD; and as GOD was pleased to send me out first, and to enlighten me first, so I think he still continues to do it.[25]

How is this statement to be evaluated?

First of all, it would be a mistake to underrate Whitefield's flair for the dramatic as he was first and foremost a *preacher*. Thus, the use of hyperbole to make a dramatic polemical point should not come as a surprise. The fact that Whitefield adds colour to his argument by drawing a parallel between himself and the apostle Paul in Galatians 1 would suggest that it may be that he is downplaying Calvin's influence on his thinking in order to highlight the dominant shaping effect of Scripture. Thus, like Paul he had not learned his theology from 'mere men,' it had come from God's own revelation in Scripture. Hood is surely correct in claiming that, 'Whitefield may not have read Calvin in his Oxford days, but the "never read" statement cannot be relied upon too heavily.'[26]

Secondly, there is evidence that after 1740 Whitefield did make some attempt to wrestle with Calvin, but only on an occasional basis. And so Clarkson comes to the conclusion that he viewed Calvin as 'a prominent person in Christian history, not as a theologian.'[27] In 1741, Whitefield writes that he had 'several of Calvin's books.'[28] And again, with some rhetorical flourish echoing the Apostle Paul in 1 Corinthians 3, he relativizes the influence and importance of Calvin by stating, 'You remember what I have often told you about Calvin ... But what is Calvin or what is Luther? Let us look above names and parties; let JESUS, the ever-loving, the ever-lovely Jesus, be our all in all.'[29]

Hood concludes that this and similar statements parallel the 1740 'never read Calvin' statement, and goes on to offer a more cautious assessment, that 'whilst it cannot be shown that Whitefield had read Calvin prior to 1740, neither can the letter to Wesley be used in evidence that he had not.'[30]

---

[25] Whitefield, *Works*, Vol. 1, p 232.
[26] Hood, 'I never read Calvin', p 17.
[27] Clarkson, *Whitefield and Welsh Calvinist Methodism*, pp 24-25.
[28] Whitefield, *Works*, Vol. 1, Letter CCLXVIII, p 283.
[29] Whitefield, *Works*, Vol. 2, Letter DCCCCXII, p 433.
[30] Hood, 'I never read Calvin', p 17.

2.4. *Preached Calvinism*

George Whitefield's Calvinism was *preached* Calvinism and so *applied*. Whilst the 'thunder and the lightning' of Whitefield's preaching cannot be recaptured, we can still hear echoes of that thunder and perceive glimpses of the lightening which accompanied such unparalleled preaching through his sermons preserved in print. It is possible to trace the 'golden chain' of Romans 8 referred to by Helm, in order to demonstrate that Whitefield was indeed a doctrinal Calvinist, that the doctrines of grace adorned his preaching as he sought by his preaching to adorn the doctrines of grace, or to be more precise, adorn his gracious Saviour. Whitefield was aware that all doctrinal points were inter-related, operating in mutual support so that the whole is greater than the sum of the individual parts.

We now turn to give samples of preached Calvinism which illustrate the 'five-pointed' nature of Whitefield's Calvinistic framework (Total depravity, Unconditional Election, Limited or Particular Atonement, Irresistible Grace and Perseverance of the Saints), and consider how such beliefs undergirded Whitefield's preaching and gave it convictional power.

The federal covenantal framework of Whitefield's beliefs is wonderfully illustrated by his sermon, 'The Seed of the Woman and the Seed of the Serpent', based on Genesis 3:15, and published in 1742.[31]

> It is only a declaration of a free gift of salvation through Jesus Christ our Lord. God the Father and God the Son had entered into a covenant concerning the salvation of the elect from all eternity, wherein God the Father promised that if the Son would offer his soul a sacrifice for sin, he should see his seed ... The truth is this: God, as a reward of Christ's sufferings, promised to give the elect faith and repentance, in order to bring them to eternal life. And both these and everything else necessary for their everlasting happiness and infallibility secured to them in this promise ... [P]eople should be taught that the Lord Jesus Christ, was the Second Adam with whom the Father entered into covenant for fallen man. That they can do nothing of or for themselves and should therefore come to God, beseeching them to give them faith, by which they will then show forth by their works, out of love and gratitude to the ever

---

[31] Lee Gatiss (ed.), *The Sermons of George Whitefield*. Vol. 1 (Wheaton, IL: Crossway, 2012), pp 41-62.

> blessed Jesus, their most glorious Redeemer, for what he has done for their souls. This is a consistent scriptural scheme. Without holding this, we must run into one of those two bad extremes, I mean Antinomianism on the one hand, and Arminianism on the other. From both of which may the good Lord deliver us.[32]

This sermon pinpoints the view that the eternal covenant made between the members of the Trinity inextricably involves particular election and effectual calling. 'The truth is this,' said Whitefield, 'God, as a reward of Christ's sufferings, promised to give the elect faith and repentance ....'[33]

Such an election is with specific people in mind, those whom God 'foreknew'. Thus Whitefield remarks in 'The Righteousness of Christ an Everlasting Righteousness':

> when Christ's righteousness is here spoken of we are to understand "Christ's obedience and death", all that Christ has suffered for an elect world, for all that will believe on him ... Hence it is, that the Lord Jesus when he calls his elect people up to heaven, says, "Come, ye blessed of my father." And what follows? "Receive the kingdom prepared for you." How long? "From the foundations of the world." All that we receive in time, all the streams that come to our souls, are but so many streams flowing from that inexhaustible fountain, God's electing sovereign, God's distinguishing, God's everlasting love.[34]

Also note how Whitefield in this sermon holds together without apology or embarrassment the twin doctrines of God's electing sovereignty and human responsibility, for all that *will* believe on him.

The doctrine of election magnifies God's majesty as well as his mercy. Here, we see Whitefield doing precisely what Wesley said he unceasingly wished to do, 'making Christ as high as possible.' But the coherence of the golden chain of Romans 8 can only be held together with the complementary doctrine of grace, namely, that man is to be seen as 'low as possible'. Not that this was a contrived and, therefore, false assessment of man's condition, but one to which both Scripture and experience testify. In the sermon 'Walking with God' he says,

> Perhaps it may seem a hard saying to some but our own experience daily proves what the scriptures in many places assert, that the

---

[32] Gatiss (ed.), *Sermons*, Vol. 1, pp 57-58.
[33] Gatiss (ed.), *Sermons*, Vol. 1, p 57.
[34] Gatiss (ed.), *Sermons*, Vol. 1, p 290.

carnal mind, the mind of the unconverted natural man, nay, the mind of the regenerate, so far as any part of him remains unrenewed, is enmity, not only an enemy but enmity itself, against God so that it is not subject to the law of God neither can it be.[35]

If anyone believed in Total Depravity, it was George Whitefield!

It is the dead spiritual state of unregenerate man, whose state of mind *is* enmity (Romans 8:7), which makes effectual calling a necessary condition of a person's personal salvation. Thus we have Whitefield in his magisterial sermon, 'The Potter and the Clay':

> If it be inquired who is to be the potter? And by whose agency this marred clay is to be formed into another vessel? ... I answer, not by mere dint and force of moral persuasion. This is good in its place. And I am so far from thinking, that Christian preachers should not make use of rational arguments and motives in their sermons, that I cannot think they are fit to preach at all, who either cannot, or will not use them. All this we readily grant. But at the same time, I would as soon go to yonder church-yard and attempt to raise the dead carcasses, with a 'come forth', as to preach to dead souls, did I not hope for some superior power to make the word effectual to the designed end. ... Neither is this change to be wrought by the power of our own free-will. This is an idol everywhere set up but we dare not fall down and worship it. "No man (says Christ) can come to me, unless the Father draw him." Our own free-will, if improved, may restrain us from the commission of many evils and put us in the way of conversion. But after exerting our utmost efforts (and we are bound in duty to exert them) we shall find the words of our own church articles to be true, that "man since the Fall hath no power to turn to God". ... I inform you, that this heavenly potter, this blessed agent, is the Almighty Spirit of God, the Holy Ghost, the third person in the most adorable Trinity, co-essential with the Father and the Son.[36]

In his preaching, Whitefield drove home to his hearers the rationale for the need for effectual grace,

> All that Christ has done, all that Christ hath suffered, all Christ's active obedience, all Christ's passive obedience, will do us no good, unless by the Spirit of God, it is brought into our souls. As one

---

[35] Gatiss (ed.), *Sermons*, Vol. 1, p 65.
[36] Gatiss (ed.), *Sermons*, Vol. 1, pp 258-259.

expresses it, 'An unapplied Christ is no Christ at all.' To hear of Christ dying for sinners will only increase your damnation, will only sink you deeper into hell, unless you have ground to say, by a work of grace wrought in our hearts, that the Lord Jesus hath brought this home to us.[37]

This is a clear example of what Dr D Martyn Lloyd-Jones called 'logic on fire.'[38]

It was the deeply held belief in God's power to give life to the spiritually dead that enabled Whitefield to engage in evangelism with such confidence and tireless energy. Otherwise, to call upon people to repent would be as foolhardy as preaching to the residents of a graveyard!

For Whitefield, election also implied particular atonement as we see from this extract from his sermon, 'The Good Shepherd':

If you belong to Jesus Christ, he is speaking of you; for says he, "I know my sheep." "I know them;" what does that mean? Why, he knows their number, he knows their names, he knows every one for whom he died; and if there were to be one missing for whom Christ died, God the Father would send him down again from heaven to fetch him ... O come, come, see what it is to have eternal life; do not refuse it; haste, sinner, haste away: may the great, the good Shepherd, draw your souls.[39]

This demonstrates that Whitefield did not draw unwarranted conclusions from his doctrines of grace, lapsing into a kind of fatalism that would not require any appeal to men and women to surrender their lives to Christ in faith. In a letter to Wesley dated in 1741, he says, 'Though I hold particular election, yet I offer Jesus freely to every individual soul.'[40] As seen in the extract from his sermon, 'The Potter and the Clay', Whitefield was aware that God had instituted certain means to achieve certain ends, hence the use of rational arguments to persuade. In other words, Gospel proclamation is needed to secure Gospel salvation. This, though necessary, is not sufficient to bring a person to a saving knowledge of Christ. There is needed the agency of

---

[37] Gatiss (ed.), *Sermons*, Vol. 1, p 295.
[38] 'What is preaching? Logic on fire! Eloquent reason!' D. Martyn Lloyd-Jones, *Preaching and Preachers.* (London: Hodder and Stoughton, 1971), p 97.
[39] Gatiss (ed.), *Sermons*, Vol. 2, p 455.
[40] Haykin, *The Revived Puritan*, p 145.

'the Almighty Spirit of God.' However, being aware of his hearers lacking such faith, Whitefield did not hesitate to appeal to them to seek God for it: 'Beg of God to give you faith. And, if the Lord gives you that, you will receive Christ, with his righteousness and his all.'[41]

In part, it was the positive nature of the doctrines of grace which of necessity led Whitefield to draw attention to the negative aspects of their opposite – Arminianism. Thus in his sermon, 'The Lord our Righteousness', Whitefield, in order to make a pastoral application rather than a polemical point, unpacks the consequences of Arminianism which he saw as being theologically disastrous and pastorally ruinous. He says,

> Being once born under the covenant of works, it is natural for us all to have recourse to a covenant of works for our everlasting salvation. And we have contracted such devilish pride by our fall from God that we would, if not wholly, yet in part at least, to glory in being the cause of our own salvation. We cry out against popery and that very justly. But we are all Papists, at least I am sure, we are all Arminians by nature. And therefore, no wonder so many natural men embrace that scheme.[42]

He later goes on to say of Christ's particular atonement,

> In that nature he obeyed and thereby fulfilled the whole moral law in our stead and also died a painful death upon the cross and thereby became a curse for, or instead of, those whom the Father had given him.[43]

But, he expostulates,

> Arminian principles being antichristian principles, always did and always will lead to antichristian practices. And never was there a reformation brought about in the church but by preaching the doctrine of imputed righteousness ... But Satan (and no wonder that his servant imitate him) often transforms himself into an angel of light and therefore (such perverse things will infidelity and Arminian make men speak) in order to dress their objections in the best colours, some urge, 'That our Saviour preached no such doctrine; that in the Sermon on the Mount, he mentions only

---

[41] Gatiss (ed.), *Sermons*, Vol. 1, p 279.
[42] Gatiss (ed.), *Sermons*, Vol. 1, p 262.
[43] Gatiss (ed.), *Sermons*, Vol. 1, p 265.

morality' and consequently the doctrine of imputed righteousness falls wholly on the ground.... For, if the whole personal righteousness of Jesus Christ be not the sole cause of my acceptance with God, if any work done or foreseen by God as an inducing, impulsive cause of acquitting my soul from guilt, then I have somewhat whereof I may glory in myself. Now boasting is excluded in the great work of Redemption.[44]

Wishing for his hearers to see the errors of false paths to belief, Whitefield also made it his business to enable them to see the positive value of right belief. Whitefield's preaching was always intensely practical, designed to elicit a response of the whole person. Therefore, not surprisingly, he glories in the doctrine of the perseverance of the saints:

> [T]hanks be to God for that divine text, "There is now no condemnation to them that are in Christ Jesus." Though God's people may fall foully. And though many of us are full of doubts and fears and say, "One day I shall fall by the hands of Saul" however your poor souls may be harassed, yet no wicked devil, nor your own depraved heart, shall be able to separate you from the love of God. God has loved you, God has fixed his heart upon you and having loved his own, he loves them unto the end. The Lord of life and of glory, the blessed Lord Jesus, will never cease loving you, till he hath loved and brought you to heaven when he will rejoice and say, "Behold me, O my Father and the dear children thou hast given me; thou gavest them to me; thine they were, I have brought them with my blood, I have won them with my sword and with my bow and I now will wear them as so many jewels of my crown."[45]

Elsewhere he explicitly links election with the security of all the blessings a believer receives in Christ,

> But what shall I say? Election is a mystery that shines with such resplendent brightness, that, to make use of the words of one who has drunk deeply of electing love, it dazzles the weak eyes even of some of God's children; however, though they know it not, all the blessing they receive, all the privileges they do or will enjoy, through Jesus Christ, flow from the everlasting love of God the Father.[46]

---

[44] Gatiss (ed.), *Sermons*, Vol. 1, pp 266-267.
[45] Gatiss (ed.), *Sermons*, Vol. 1, pp 291-292.
[46] Gatiss (ed.), *Sermons*, Vol. 2, pp 212-213.

As is evident from this sermon, Whitefield had a concern that such doctrines of grace be 'felt' and enjoyed as much as being assented to and believed. He wrote from Philadelphia in 1739,

> Oh the excellency of the doctrine of election, and of the saints' final perseverance, to those who are truly sealed by the Spirit of promise! I am persuaded, till a man comes to believe and feel these important truths, he cannot come out of himself; but when convinced of these, and assured of the application of them to his own heart, he then walks by faith indeed, not in himself but in the Son of God, who died and gave himself for him. Love, not fear, constrains him to obedience.[47]

To John Wesley in 1740, he opened his heart: '[Of] the doctrine of election, and the final perseverance of those that are truly in Christ, I am ten thousand times more convinced of, if possible, then when I saw you last.'[48] Furthermore, it was these doctrines of grace, holding together in an unbreakable unity the golden chain of Romans 8 which was a sustaining tonic to his own soul: 'Surely I am safe, because put into his almighty arms. Though I may fall, yet I shall not utterly be cast away. The Spirit of the Lord Jesus will hold, and uphold me.'[49]

2.5. Conclusion

From this survey there are three characteristics of George Whitefield's Calvinistic preaching which can serve as lessons for preachers today who would see themselves as standing within this tradition.

The first is that it is *convinced* preaching. Whitefield held to the doctrines of grace as a matter of deep conviction, convinced in his own mind and heart that these were nothing less than the teachings of Jesus himself. Whitefield is sometimes portrayed as a great dramatist in his

---

[47] Haykin, *The Revived Puritan*, pp 71-72.
[48] Haykin, *The Revived Puritan*, p 113.
[49] Haykin, *The Revived Puritan*, p 76.

preaching.[50] But the emotions displayed were not those of an actor of the stature of Garrick; they more closely resembled those of the Saviour, who himself believed that, "No one can come to me unless the Father who sent me draws him" (John 10:44), and "Everyone who listens to the Father and learns from him will come to me" (John 6:45). Those were the convictions shared by Whitefield and which were released through his preaching.

Secondly, Whitefield's sermons display *confident* preaching. Having a realistic estimation of man's spiritual inability to repent, Whitefield had an equally clear estimation of God's ability to regenerate. God's electing love displayed on the cross, worked out in regenerate hearts only to be consummated in glory, gave Whitefield confidence to preach to all without despairing and to continue to preach without tiring. The encouragement of God's electing purpose given by God to strengthen the apostle Paul could equally apply to Whitefield: "I have many people in this city"(Acts 18:10).

Thirdly, this was *convicting* preaching. The great realities of heaven and hell, passionately held and powerfully proclaimed, together with the liberating force of the doctrines of grace energised by God's Spirit, led to deep conviction on the part of many of Whitefield's hearers. It was by presenting man at his lowest and Christ at his highest that many were left not only cognisant of their desperate plight but *feeling* it. Then, having come face to face with their own need and inability, when the doctrines of grace were presented they were welcomed in all their life transforming, God honouring, glory.

---

[50] Stout says 'the key to understanding him is "the amalgam of preaching and acting." Whitefield was "the consummate actor." "The fame he sought was ... the actor's command performance on centre stage." "Whitefield was not content simply to talk about the New Birth; he had to sell it with all the dramatic artifice of a huckster." "Tears became Whitefield's ... psychological gesture." "Whitefield became an actor-preacher, as opposed to a scholar-preacher." And, of course, this last statement is true, in one sense. He was an actor-preacher as opposed to a scholar-preacher. He was not a Jonathan Edwards. He preached totally without notes, and his traveling pulpit was more of a tiny stage than it was a traditional pulpit. Unlike most of the preachers in his day he was full of action when he preached. ... [Yet] Whitefield's "acting" was not acting in the theatrical sense at all' (John Piper, 'I Will Not Be a Velvet-Mouthed Preacher!' The Life and Ministry of George Whitefield: Living and Preaching as Though God Were Real (Because He is)'; available at http://www.desiringgod.org/messages/i-will-not-be-a-velvet-mouthed-preacher [accessed 12.08.2015]). That Whitefield was emotional in his preaching doesn't mean that he engaged in emotional*ism* as might an actor in order to elicit a response from his audience.

In an age of *PowerPoint* sermons and 'what would Jesus do' sound-bites, which do not seem to produce the effect of the sermons preached by Whitefield, perhaps ministers today would do well to return to 'the old paths' by holding on to and holding out the doctrines of grace which Whitefield proclaimed to such great effect in his day.

2.6. Sources

Clarkson, George E. *George Whitefield and Welsh Calvinist Methodism*. Lampeter: Edwin Mellen Press, 1996.
Dallimore, Arnold A. *George Whitefield: The Life and Times of the Great Evangelist of the 18th Century Revival*. Volume 2. Banner of Truth Trust, 1980.
Gatiss (ed.), Lee. *The Sermons of George Whitefield*. Volume 1. Wheaton, IL: Crossway, 2012.
_____. *The Sermons of George Whitefield*. Volume 2. Wheaton, IL: Crossway, 2012.
Haykin, Michael A. G. *The Revived Puritan: The Spirituality of George Whitefield*. Dundas, Ontario: Joshua Press, 2000.
Helm, Paul. 'The Many Shades of Calvinism',http://paulhelmsdeep.blogspot.com/2011/03/many-shades-of-calvinism.html [accessed 12.08.2015].
Hood, Jared C. '"I never read Calvin"; George Whitefield, a Calvinist Untimely Born', *Churchman* 125/1 (2011), pp. 7-20.
Jackson (ed.), Thomas. *The Works of John Wesley*. Volume 6. Grand Rapids, MI: Baker Book House, 1986.
Jones, David C. White, Eryn M. and Schlenther, Boyd S. *The Elect Methodists: Calvinistic Methodism in England and Wales, 1735-1811*. Cardiff: The University of Wales Press, 2012.
Lloyd-Jones, D. Martyn. *Preaching and Preachers*. London: Hodder and Stoughton, 1971.
Olson, Roger E. *Against Calvinism*. Grand Rapids, MI: Zondervan, 2011.
Packer, J.I 'The Reformational Revivalism of George Whitefield,' in *Honouring the People of God, The Collected Shorter Writings of J.I. Packer*. Volume 2. Carlisle: Paternoster, 1999.
Stout, Harry S. *The Divine Dramatist: George Whitefield and the Rise of Modern Evangelicalism*. Grand Rapids, MI: Eerdmans, 1991.
Tinker, Melvin. *The Anglican Evangelical Crisis*. Christian Focus Publications, 1995.
_____. *Intended for Good: The Providence of God*. Nottingham: IVP, 2012.
Tyerman, Luke. *The Life of the Revd George Whitefield, B.A., of Pembroke College, Oxford*. Volume I. London: Hodder and Stoughton, 1876.
Whitefield, George. *The Letters of George Whitefield, 1734-42*. Edinburgh: Banner of Truth, 1976.
_____. *The Works of George Whitefield*. Oswestry: Quinta Press, 2000.

3. The Pastoral Sermons of George Whitefield
by Victor Emma-Adamah and Phumezo Masango

3.1. George Whitefield as 'Pastor'?

The title of this chapter immediately presents itself for debate and questioning – The pastoral sermons of George Whitefield? Can Whitefield, the evangelist-revivalist par excellence and celebrity itinerant preacher, properly speaking, be considered to have pastoral sermons, being that he was constantly on the move and did not have any prolonged pastoral oversight of a congregation? In what is this qualification, 'pastoral,' to be reckoned – does it qualify something of the *nature* of the sermon or rather the *context* of its delivery? What makes one sermon pastoral as opposed to another? In the following discussion, these questions will be explored in due course.

3.2. Introduction

The history-defining moment of the life and ministry of George Whitefield (1714-70) can hardly be exaggerated. This, not only within the confines of Christian theology and practice, his central role in birthing important strands that would shape the evangelical movement till today, his significance in the waves of revival and the reawakening of authentic religion in Britain and America and beyond, as has been amply attested in the literature, but even beyond these, to his significance in defining the consciousness and spiritual élan that would result in the founding of a whole nation – as a historian recently captioned it, Whitefield was 'America's spiritual founding father'.[1]

For all this influence, arguably, the singular factor that distinguished George Whitefield, if any such must be reckoned, is to be found in his sermons and the dramatic, mesmerizing presence that accompanied their delivery, not to mention the extraordinary spiritual power that left many in tears and in trance-like states after his preaching. Everywhere he went masses thronged to see and hear him speak, and were convicted and converted; revivals and awakenings broke

---

[1] Thomas S. Kidd, *George Whitefield: America's Spiritual Founding Father* (New Haven: Yale University Press, 2014).

out, and the state of religion in whole towns was improved remarkably.[2] In the well-known 1740 account of the Connecticut farmer, Nathan Cole: 'hearing him [Whitefield] preach, gave me a heart wound; by God's blessing: my old foundation was broken up, and I saw that my righteousness would not save me.'[3]

But, granted his successes in the preaching ministry, in the consideration of the pastoral angle or value of his sermons, some difficulties emerge. Harry Stout, reflecting on possible factors for Whitefield's epochal success in comparison with traditional pastors of the same time, would comment:

> [H]is experience appears more analogous to the actor on tour than to the settled preacher. Unlike ministers who preached only once or twice a week and could more easily separate their "roles" as pastor, father, husband, and community pillar, Whitefield lived in his own self-embracing world of dramatic re-enactment.[4]

In this, Stout gave voice to something that has always been taken for granted as a given of Whitefield's ministry in general – that by virtue of the intensely itinerant nature of his ministry, the extremely active schedule he operated, and the wide geographical expanse over which his preaching played out (this, without the benefit of modern transportation and communication), he practically pioneered an altogether novel category of ministerial identity and *modus operandi*. That is, the itinerant, inter-denominational, revivalist-evangelist commanding mass public appeal; this in contradistinction from the settled, long-term *pastor* (the original meaning of shepherd) over a local flock. As such, there seems to be a certain transitoriness that necessarily characterizes his itinerant ministry – this, particularly from the perspective of the numerous different audiences he engaged – and perhaps a perceptibly ad hoc nature to his sermons: often prepared during travels. As such,

---

[2] As Jonathan Edwards would testify after the series of sermons preached in 1740 by Whitefield in the former's Northampton congregation: 'Mr. Whitefield's sermons were suitable to the circumstances of the town... Immediately after this the minds of the people in general appeared more engaged in religion, shewing a greater forwardness to make religion the subject of their conversation, and to meet frequently together for religious purposes, and to embrace all opportunities to hear the Word preached' (*The Works of Jonathan Edwards* Vol. 4 (New Haven: Yale University Press, 1957-2008), p 545).

[3] Michael J. Crawford (ed.), 'The Spiritual Travels of Nathan Cole,' *William and Mary Quarterly*, 3rd ser., 33, no. 1 (Jan 1976): 92. Taken from Kidd, *George Whitefield*, p 131.

[4] Harry Stout, *The Divine Dramatist: George Whitefield and the Rise of Modern Evangelicalism*, (Grand Rapids, MI: Wm. B. Eerdmans, 1991), p 106.

Whitefield's ministry in general, it might be expected, would lack the sense of ongoing discipleship, pastoral care and oversight characteristic of a pastor's long-term engagement with the spiritual and physical needs of a local congregation.

As a result, even his sermons appear to have been tailored to deliver the essentials of the gospel in single potent dosages, as it were, given the limited time he had with audiences; sermons which, without any watering down of the gospel (*au contraire!* for Whitefield), were simple, accessible and designed for mass consumption by audiences of widely varying spiritual and intellectual abilities. Sarah Pierpont Edward's assessment of Whitefield's preaching after the itinerant's visit to her husband's (Jonathan) Northampton church in 1740 is incisive:

> He makes less of the doctrines than our American preachers generally do and aims more at affecting the heart. He is a born orator.... It is wonderful to see what a spell he casts over an audience by proclaiming the simplest truths of the Bible. I have seen upwards of a thousand people hang on his words with breathless silence, broken only by an occasional half-suppressed sob.[5]

This early recognition and portrait of George Whitefield's sermons and ministry as essentially evangelistic and revivalist in nature is one that would stand out and be reinforced over and again during the course of his career. Whitefield himself, from the thousands of sermons that he preached, gives incontrovertible evidence that the 'evangelistic genre' was his area of specialization, as it were. 'O Sinners,' George Whitefield cried earnestly as he preached to the crowd gathered in the High Church Yard of Glasgow on the 12th of September 1741,

> I would fain turn to preach the Comforts of the Gospel, but I must speak a little more of the Law to you; ye are hanging over the fiery Furnace, over Hell-fire, by a single Thread of this Life; God Almighty knows but this may be the last Time ye shall hear this Word, and out of Christ ye will find God to be to you a consuming Fire... *Indeed it is*

---

[5] See Stout, *The Divine Dramatist*, p 127; Also, Randy Petersen, *The Printer and the Preacher: Ben Franklin, George Whitefield, and the Surprising Friendship That Invented America* (Nashville, TN.: Thomas Nelson, 2015), p 169; David S. Lovejoy, *Religious Enthusiasm and the Great Awakening* (Englewood Cliffs, N.J.: Prentice-Hall, 1969), pp 33-34. To show that Sarah did not put forward this appraisal as a negative impression of Whitefield's preaching, she would conclude, saying, 'A prejudiced person, I know, might say that this is all theatrical artifice and display; but not so will anyone think who has seen and known him.'

out of Love and Sincere Affection to your Soul I speak so.[6]

This sermon that pulsates with evangelistic fervour was, surprisingly, delivered largely to very mature believers and clergymen in Scotland on the theme of the duty of the minister. Whitefield powerfully proclaims an evangelistic message of regeneration and the need for heart-felt conversion, and this, as he avows, was motivated by his love and affection for the well-being of his listeners' souls. The nexus of evangelistic theological themes, then, – new birth, conversion, regeneration, new creation – easily dominate Whitefield's ministry, and seem directly to inform other themes of his sermons, irrespective of the preaching context.

The largely itinerant nature of Whitefield's ministry makes him more suited to the image of the gifted, charismatic revivalist who excels at pioneering and planting spiritual seeds, but less gifted at watering and nurturing those seeds; as the contrasting image of the settled, 'faithful' country pastor would suggest. By all indications, Whitefield himself understood his ministry role to be concerned primarily with seed planting. In a letter to John Wesley in March 1739, Whitefield would implore the Methodist founder to come to Bristol 'and water what God has enabled me to plant.'[7] In the absence of an image of Whitefield fitting the role of the provincial pastor – one serving as shepherd over a community of faithful believers, and tending regularly to their spiritual and life needs – it becomes difficult to cast his sermons in that light pertaining properly to the pastor-teacher whose sermons are aimed at the consistent teaching, reproof, correction and training in righteousness of his congregants.

It is clear, then, that Whitefield's sermons cannot be spoken of as 'pastoral' in the same sense that, say, Jonathan Edwards' sermons may be considered. But it seems unreasonable to reject outright that his sermons were of ongoing pastoral value to many, even given the dynamic nature of his ministry. But, the question then must be posed: In what sense can his sermons therefore be seen as pastoral?

In light of the foregoing, then, the remainder of the discussion will attempt to provide a possible way of reckoning Whitefield's sermons as pastoral, and then proceed to give a sampling of these sermons.

---

[6] George Whitefield, *The Duty of a Gospel Minister* (Glasgow: Robert Shaw, 1741), p 30 (emphasis added).
[7] Whitefield to John Wesley, March 3, 1739, in Baker, ed., *Works of John Wesley*, 25:611. Taken from Kidd, *George Whitefield*, p 70.

3.3. 'The one thing needful': the care of souls as paradigm for Whitefield's 'pastoral' ministry

Even given an itinerant and dynamic ministry, perhaps George Whitefield's own understanding of his role vis-à-vis the millions of souls that heard him preach over his lifetime, would give insights into the pastoral dimension of his sermons. What is the fundamental or core missional self-understanding that holds the diverse aspects of Whitefield's ministry together?

A sermon of Whitefield's – preached on May 19th 1739 on Kennington Common, a few months prior to his first journey to America and the explosion of his itinerant evangelistic ministry – gives a clear picture of his overarching mission and self-understanding as a gospel minister. Its title aptly captures the fundamental nature of this perspective: *The Care of the Soul Urged as the One Thing Needful*.[8] Taking Luke 10:42 as his text, Whitefield describes the background story of Jesus in the house of Lazarus, Mary and Martha in Bethany. He draws attention to Jesus' identification of the essence of his own ministry as the concern for the soul and its spiritual state, even in the face of the lure of entertainment and distraction. As Whitefield presents it, Jesus' gentle rebuke of Martha's preoccupation with the physical demands of entertainment and hospitality represent 'a kind of aphorism, or wise and weighty sentence' that encapsulates the emphasis of Christ's ministry as a whole: 'Martha, Martha, thou art careful and troubled about many things but *one thing is needful*. And Mary has chosen that good part, which shall not be taken away from her.'[9] This one thing needful, identified as it is with the care of the soul, far from being a reductionism of all Christian enterprise to spiritual concerns, is rather identified by Whitefield as the 'one sacred principle of divine life' from which the multifaceted nature of the Christian as a whole springs. As he summarizes it,

> The care of the soul is of so comprehensive a nature, that everything truly worthy of our regard may be considered as included in it, or subservient to it.[10]

---

[8] Lee Gatiss (ed.), *The Sermons of George Whitefield*. Volume 2 (Wheaton, IL: Crossway, 2012), p 7.
[9] Gatiss (ed.), *Sermons*, Vol. 2, p 8.
[10] Gatiss (ed.), *Sermons*, Vol. 2, p 12.

Hence, when Whitefield speaks of the care of the soul as *the* one thing needful, he understands not the neglect of other anthropological dimensions, but the spiritual nurture and care of the soul as the *perspective* under which every concern of the Christian life is addressed.

But how does he conceive of the parts and elements of this 'care of souls'? Most generally understood:

> The care of the soul, implies a readiness to hear the words of Christ, to seat ourselves with Mary at his feet and to receive both the law and the gospel from his mouth. It supposes, that we learn from this divine teacher the worth of our souls, their danger and their remedy. And that we become above all things solicitous about their salvation. That, heartily repenting of all our sins and cordially believing the everlasting gospel, we receive the Lord Jesus Christ for righteousness and life, resting our souls on the value of his atonement and the efficacy of his grace. It imports, the sincere dedication of ourselves to the service of God and a faithful adherence to it, notwithstanding all oppositions arising from inward corruptions, or outward temptations. And a resolute perseverance in the way of gospel dependence, 'till we receive the end of our faith in our complete salvation.[11]

In what reads like a creedal statement, Whitefield plots a rich scheme that comprises the moment from a sinner's initial hearing of the gospel and conversion, the ongoing life of sanctification as a disciple of Christ, to the glorious consummation of salvation. The soul of man, as Whitefield qualifies it, is a 'matter of universal concern,' 'of highest importance,' and a thing 'comprehensive in nature.' To further show that by this priority on the care of the soul he is not referring to life as an ethereal spiritualism, he emphasizes that it 'comprehends all the lovely and harmonious band of social and human virtues...[and] requires a care of society, a care of our bodies and of our temporal concerns.'[12] However, all these from the perspective of their being 'regulated, directed, and animated' properly by the believer's progress in the divine life.

Whitefield would then go on to identify this care of the soul with specific doctrines in Scriptures: doctrines such as 'regeneration' or 'new creation,' 'faith' or 'receiving Christ and believing on him,' 'the Fear of

---

[11] Gatiss (ed.), *Sermons*, Vol. 2, pp 8-9.
[12] Gatiss (ed.), *Sermons*, Vol. 2, p 12.

God,' and 'the great work of God.' These doctrines for Whitefield capture the operation of God in the life of a person, and are laid out in Trinitarian formula: *regeneration* is the work of God the Father's efficacious grace; *faith*, as in the New Testament, entails reception and belief in Christ; and the *great work of God* in the believer is produced by the Holy Spirit.[13]

The care of the soul, as the one thing needful, therefore, for Whitefield, becomes shorthand for the life trajectory of the Christian experience, and the spiritual fountain from which that experience springs, and it is encapsulated by the biblical doctrines of 'Regeneration,' 'faith' or 'the Fear of God,' among others – doctrines that were particular highlights of his sermons. It follows from this that Whitefield sees his efforts at preaching a message centred on regeneration, faith in Christ, and the divine life, far from merely being means of 'entry', as it were, into the Christian life, but as encompassing and undergirding the entire well-being of the Christian. As such, his emphasis on conversion must not only be reckoned in terms of evangelism, but within a more general scope of Whitefield's preoccupation for the spiritual health of the multitudes that gathered to listen to him – the care of the soul as the one thing needful.

We may now finish off the portrait of Whitefield's perspective on his ministry as 'pastoral'. From the foregoing, Whitefield's ministry may be seen as driven essentially by what is readily identified as a pastoral heart and concern for the care of souls, yet executed predominantly within a mode of open-air, itinerant, evangelistic preaching. If this is the case, one ought to look at his sermons, among other things, of course, with an eye to discerning the undergirding pastoral motivation. While one may not talk of George Whitefield as 'pastor', nor consider his sermons from the perspective of the teaching pastor with ongoing oversight of the spiritual matters of congregational life, yet one may speak of Whitefield as '*pastoral*', and eminently so. Pastoral, as such, in his understanding that the care of souls, the cultivation of the divine life becomes the foundation proper for overall health of the Christian life. Whitefield saw his vocation as a minister in the light of his being entrusted with the sobering task of caring for souls – a matter of eternal consequence. As he would remark soberly: 'Pardon my plainness. If it were a fable or a tale, I would endeavour to amuse you with words but I cannot do it where souls are at stake.'[14]

---

[13] Gatiss (ed.), *Sermons*, Vol. 2, p 9.
[14] Gatiss (ed.), *Sermons*, Vol. 2, p 23.

In this light, then, one may speak of a 'pastoral thrust' to Whitefield's sermons, and further explore his preaching as multifaceted applications of the 'one thing needful'. In the following sections, an attempt will be made to explore a few identified aspects of George Whitefield's sermons as laying the foundations for what has been described as his pastoral concern or thrust.

3.4. Aspects of Whitefield's sermons as pastoral

Against the backdrop sketched above, we shall explore a very select group of George Whitefield's sermons as 'pastoral sermons', relating these to the portrait of the care of the soul and the cultivation of the all-round spiritual health of the believer. These will be explored under three rubrics: (i) his sermons on true conversion and devotion; (ii) sermons addressing the believer's life in the Spirit and ongoing sanctification; (iii) sermons addressing matters of practical application and lifestyle.

Methodologically, the presentation of these sermons does not follow a strict systematic format. It has also not been particularly pertinent to the present task to explore Whitefield's sermons following a historical diachronic analysis. This survey approach, far from suggesting any insensitivity to the possibility of development and progressive maturation of his sermons over his career, is based on the appraisal of a generally consistent theological core to Whitefield's sermons.[15] From his first public sermon – delivered on June 27, 1736, and titled, *The Necessity and Benefits of Religious Society* – the core themes of conversion, Christian devotion and lifestyle are already observed. These, and cognate theological motifs, would remain fairly consistently throughout his preaching life.

3.4.1. True conversion and devotion

Central to the pastoral dimension of George Whitefield's preaching was his tireless drive to promote authentic Christian religion as a living relationship with God, and his concomitant abhorrence of empty ceremony, and the spiritually vacuous religiosity that he observed all too frequently among many clergy. He would describe the professor of such blasé religion as the one who is 'fond of the form but never experiences

---

[15] See Benjamin Dean's article, 'Whitefield's Evangelical Theology' in this present volume for an exploration of this theological core and its identification as an evangelical theology.

the power of godliness in his heart.'[16] In numerous heated exchanges, Whitefield would condemn ministers perceived to be of this lukewarm ilk – notably his dismissal of the then deceased but yet prominent latitudinarian and anti-Calvinist Anglican archbishop, John Tillotson (1630–1694) as one who 'knew no more of true Christianity than Mahomet.'[17] Whitefield would decry this poor spiritual state of ministers and, consequently, its reflection on their congregations. In a sermon to ministers, he would admonish and encourage:

> I would exhort you in the Name, and by the Mercy of the Lord Jesus Christ, to examine your Hearts, and see whether ye feel these Truths ye are preaching to your Congregations or not. It will be but poor, dry, sapless Stuff, your People will go away out of the Church as cold as they came in, except your Ministry be attended with the Power of God.[18]

No doubt, informed by his personal spiritual journey to true conversion, Whitefield was particularly aware of the dangers of unwitting self-deception in assuming conversion where in reality true rebirth had failed to take place.[19]

3.4.1.1. Regeneration

As a result of these factors, Whitefield had a heightened sensitivity to the dangers of Christian religiosity without conversion, and made the preaching of regeneration and the evangelical gospel to take centre stage in his sermons. This emphasis, however, must not be heard simply on an evangelistic registry, but also on one of spiritual formation – Whitefield's holistic aim of cultivating and nurturing mature spiritual life and devotion.

In a sermon – informatively captioned *The Almost Christian* – preached at Saint John Wapping in 1738, still at the very early stages of his ministry, Whitefield would explore 'ineffectualness, danger, absurdity, and uneasiness which attends those who are but almost

---

[16] Gatiss (ed.), *Sermons*, Vol. 2, p 202.
[17] George Whitefield to a friend in London, Jan 18, 1740 in *Letters of Whitefield*, 505-6. Taken from Kidd, *George Whitefield*, p 107.
[18] Whitefield, *Duty of a Gospel Minister*, p 10.
[19] For biographical accounts of Whitefield's conversion, see George Whitefield, *A Short Account of God's Dealings with the Reverend Mr. George Whitefield* (London, 1740); Kidd, *George Whitefield*, pp 20-37; L. Tyerman, *The Life of Rev. George Whitefield*, Vol. 1 (London: Hodder and Stoughton, 1876), pp 14-34.

Christian.'[20] Whitefield here considers Paul's witness of his own conversion and defence of Christianity before the Gentile governor Festus and King Agrippa in Acts 26. In the biblical account, although King Agrippa was particularly moved by Paul's preaching and made some mental ascent to its content, in a moment of transparency he confesses: 'Paul, almost thou persuadest me to be a Christian.'[21] Whitefield unpacks this confession to illustrate the deceptiveness of mistaking a person's receptivity of the gospel message for evidence of genuine piety:

> All do not thus disbelieve our report, yet amongst those who gladly receive the word and confess that we speak the words of truth and soberness, there are so few, who arrive at any higher degree of piety than that of Agrippa... I cannot but think it highly necessary to warn my dear hearers of the danger of such a state.[22]

Whitefield would go on to sketch a portrait of who this 'almost Christian' referred to within the context of his sermon audience. For the field preacher, this almost Christian was not one lacking in the performance of the rituals or emblems of religion, but rather one who is 'very cautious how he goes too far in it [religion].'[23] This polite, detached, moralistic religion, as Whitefield saw it in his day, was what he labelled simply as 'natural,' and therefore tantamount to un-conversion. Such religion lacked 'the power of godliness in [one's] heart.'[24]

Whitefield further assesses the lamentable construal of religion as denominational allegiances, moralism and activism: that these 'false notions' had become the majority opinion, such that 'few, very few acknowledge it [religion] to be what it really is, a thorough inward change of nature, a divine life, a vital participation of Jesus Christ, an union of the soul with God.'[25] No doubt, such preaching, delivered with the fire of Whitefield's oration, had for foil the cool latitudinarian piety and spiritual slumber from which the preacher tried to jolt his hearers. Whitefield, in a 1737 sermon, *On Regeneration*, would launch a targeted rebuttal against 'the groundless presumption of another class of professors, who rest in the attainment of some moral virtues and falsely

---

[20] Gatiss (ed.), *Sermons*, Vol. 2, p 201.
[21] Acts 26:28.
[22] Gatiss (ed.), *Sermons*, Vol. 2, p 201.
[23] Gatiss (ed.), *Sermons*, Vol. 2, p 202.
[24] Gatiss (ed.), *Sermons*, Vol. 2, p 203.
[25] Gatiss (ed.), *Sermons*, Vol. 2, p 205.

imagine they are good Christians, if they are just in their dealings, temperate in their diet, and do no hurt or violence to any man'[26] – an apt description for the latitudinarianism of his day.

Whitefield's sermon on regeneration gives further insight into how he understands this doctrine, and its pastoral function. In elucidating 2 Corinthians 5:17,[27] Whitefield shows regeneration to be not merely an outward profession, but to involve the inward transformation of the heart. But even further, at the essence of regeneration is the ongoing 'co-habitation' of the Holy Spirit in the believer's heart, where the Spirit is in the believer, and the believer is in Christ. Whitefield explains:

> To be in him, so as to be mystically united to him by a true and lively faith and thereby to receive spiritual virtue from him, as the members of the natural body do from the head, or the branches from the vine.[28]

Whitefield gives a particular angle and emphasis that makes the doctrine of regeneration fall very centrally within his pastoral understanding. Regeneration, as such, involves both the initial work of the spirit in new birth, *and* (this is the emphasis) a sort of spiritual ontological transformation of the believer, which is itself not a once-off work of the spirit, but ongoing in the believer's life. Regeneration, for him, is a matter of both *status* and *state*. Whitefield brings out the distinction:

> For Christians do well to consider, that there is not only a legal hindrance to our happiness, as we are breakers of God's law but also a moral impurity in our natures, which renders us incapable of enjoying heaven till some mighty change have been wrought in us.[29]

In order, then, for a believer to experience the ultimate spiritual graces prepared for him by God – which Whitefield describes as spiritual 'happiness' – regeneration is indispensable. Regeneration, therefore, on one hand, comprises that comprehensive work in Christ whereby sins are forgiven and the righteousness of Christ's perfect obedience is imputed to *sinners*; and also, the ongoing life-renewing transformation

---

[26] Gatiss (ed.), *Sermons*, Vol. 2, pp 283-4.
The pastor-theologian of Northampton, Jonathan Edwards, was involved in a similar ministry context, nurturing his congregation by admonishing them to a truly spiritual religion in a regenerated heart.
[27] 'If any man be in Christ, he is a new creature.'
[28] Gatiss (ed.), *Sermons*, Vol. 2, p 277.
[29] Gatiss (ed.), *Sermons*, Vol. 2, p 282.

whereby the Spirit sanctifies, purifies, and changes the yet corrupt natures of *believers*.[30] Cast in this broad perspective, regeneration and its cognate theological themes are, for Whitefield, equally relevant to the unsaved and to the saved – all for the purpose of the holistic cultivation and nurture of the divine life.

It thus becomes possible to see Whitefield's focused preaching on regeneration within the broader pastoral aims of the spiritual formation of believers, without thereby downplaying its ordinary evangelistic understanding. His focus on regeneration and conversion, far from being merely propaedeutic to perceived denser theological themes, or as only introductory to the Christian experience as a whole, rather falls at the centre of Whitefield's understanding of his pastoral role – his call to nurture the flock of Christ into faith and communion with God.

3.4.2. *Sanctification and the spiritual life*

If Whitefield saw regeneration holistically and endeavoured to thus nurture hearers through his sermons, he achieves this substantially by exhorting and guiding them into greater knowledge and experience of the sanctified, divine life. The glorious reality of a person's regeneration and union with Christ, for Whitefield, works itself out in the sanctifying function of the Spirit in the believer. For him, the vivid, Spirit-empowered communication of these truths through preaching represented one of the greatest tools of his pastoral ministry. This is so because only such work of sanctification results in any true transformation of believers and realizes their increased conformity to Christ. The importance of sanctification for Whitefield's pastoral preaching comes into sharper focus when it is reckoned that for him the essence of this doctrine is 'a total renovation of the whole man.'[31] For Whitefield, sanctification is not a 'spiritualism' – advocating a man-centred pursuit of earthly renunciation; nor yet is it a 'moralism,' with selfish attempts to attain commendable ethical standards. Whitefield is careful to distinguish his from the other views of sanctification considered erroneous:

> By sanctification I do not mean a bare hypocritical attendance to outward ordinances, though rightly informed Christians will think it their duty and privilege constantly to attend on all outward ordinances. Nor do I mean by sanctification a bare outward

---

[30] Gatiss (ed.), *Sermons*, Vol. 2, p 282.
[31] Gatiss (ed.), *Sermons*, Vol. 2, p 218.

reformation of a few transient convictions, or a little legal sorrow. For all this an unsanctified man may have.[32]

Rather, the focus of sanctification is the transformation of the entire human being that springs from being in Christ.

For Whitefield, some of the observable effects of this transformation include: the spiritual enlightening of the believer's understanding, the increasing conformity of their will to God's will, the redirection of their affections towards the things of God, an increased tenderness of conscience, the disciplined use of their physical bodies in pursuit of holy living, and an altogether transformed life.[33]

As a result of this transformative and comprehensive understanding, Whitefield's sermons on the sanctified life are deeply pastoral in that they admonish, guide, and encourage believers to cultivate a life of godliness manifested in every facet of personal and family life, and society at large. They aim at carrying out, using the instrument of preaching, a manifestly broad range of pastoral duties. Since the good Christian life is the direct effect of spiritual thriving, and that these two for Whitefield are organically interrelated, his sermons on themes of spiritual growth should be seen as instances of pastoral nurture.

Thus conceived, this pastoral orientation is observed in a number of instances of his sermons. In a sermon of 1740 titled *Walking with God*, Whitefield, preaching on Genesis 5:24, unpacks the reality of divine communion and spiritual growth as the all-embracing and highest goal of the Christian life – 'making progress or advances in the divine life.'[34] To show the universal application of the necessity for spiritual renewal and progress – i.e. for the unconverted, the spiritual babe, and the mature in Christ – Whitefield would describe walking with God in terms of that work of the Spirit whereby he progressively takes away from a person's heart the prevailing 'power of the enmity' against God.[35] The further this process occurs the more an individual becomes subject

---

[32] Gatiss (ed.), *Sermons*, Vol. 2, p 218.
[33] Gatiss (ed.), *Sermons*, Vol. 2, p 218.
[34] Gatiss (ed.), *Sermons*, Vol. 1, p 69.
[35] Gatiss (ed.), *Sermons*, Vol. 1, p 66.

to God's laws and conformed to Christ's image.[36] Far from advocating any notion of spiritual elitism or perfectionism, Whitefield would clarify that although all Christians stand in Christ on equal footing (all invariably are children of God), yet 'the divine life admits of decays and additions.' Even though all converted souls are made new creatures in Christ, yet conformity to the divine image, the spiritual robustness that results from communing with God is not uniform across believers.[37] The spiritual life can either be cultivated and enhanced, or neglected and left moribund, with immediate reflection in all other aspects of the individual's life. Given this position, it is this striving for divine conformity in the believer's life that becomes of paramount importance in the pastoral orientation of Whitefield's preaching. He would capture the breath of its importance for nurturing God's people in this comment:

> [W]alking with God consists especially in the fixed habitual bent of the will for God, in an habitual dependence upon his power and promise, in an habitual voluntary dedication of our all to his glory, in an habitual eyeing of his precept in all we do and in an habitual complacence in his pleasure in all we suffer.[38]

A number of Whitefield's sermons therefore give impassioned exhortations to his hearers on the need to pursue a close walk with God.

Not contenting himself, however, with exhortatory pleas, he gave pastoral guidance on practical steps to be taken in developing communion with God and furthering the spiritual life. It is important to note, vis-à-vis this exploration of Whitefield's pastoral sermons, that when he thus enjoins believers, he does not do so by disinterestedly enumerating helpful points for godly pursuit. Rather, he urges them on with the absorption and earnestness akin to a coach grooming a team, or of one having oversight and responsibility for the wellbeing of a group. In one sermon, perhaps to forestall any misinterpretation of his passionate and coach-like assertiveness in giving directives as assuming,

---

[36] Whitefield on this note is clear that this process is never achieved completely in this life. 'Observe me, I say, the prevailing power of this enmity must be taken away. For the in-being of it will never be totally removed, till we bow down our heads and give up the ghost' (Gatiss (ed.), *Sermons*, Vol. 1, p 67).
[37] Gatiss (ed.), *Sermons*, Vol. 1, p 69.
[38] Gatiss (ed.), *Sermons*, Vol. 1, p 69.

he would disclaim: 'Indeed it is out of Love and Sincere Affection to your Soul I speak so.'[39]

3.4.2.1. Guidelines for living the sanctified life

To guide the sanctified life, Whitefield emphasizes the pre-eminence of the written Word of God as the foundation for a walk with God – 'the sole rule both as to faith and practice.'[40] It is through immersion in Scripture, which is spirit and life, that believers can find nourishment for their souls. With just as much emphasis, Whitefield would identify the importance of 'secret prayer' and piety for the believer's walk with God. Prayer, he describes as 'the very breath of the new creature, the fan of the divine life, whereby the spark of holy fire, kindled in the soul by God, is not only kept in but raised into a flame.'[41] Without this element, he expounded, the warm intimacy of communion with God quickly fizzles out. Even the reading of Scripture could lose its vitality as a spiritual discipline.

Therefore, Whitefield would urge believers, giving voice to Christ's injunction, to pray without ceasing. Here he interprets Christ's command for perpetuity in prayer to mean, 'our souls [being] kept in a praying frame' – that is, a consistently prayerful heart and disposition, not an unending bodily exertion in prayer.[42] On a very practical note, being aware of the physically tasking vocations of his listeners and the constraints that such busyness imposed on praying, he would instruct them thus:

> When you are about the common business of life, be much in ejaculatory prayer and send, from time to time, short letters post to heaven upon the wings of faith.[43]

Whitefield would further enjoin his audiences to pursue meditation, which he considered a kind of silent prayer. This meditation, he elucidated, is the soul's way of 'digesting' and appropriating the spiritual virtues of God's word studied, and in that process reaches out beyond itself to God, where it is evermore inclined to apprehending something of God's glory. As such, he would commend to their

---

[39] Whitefield, *The Duty of a Gospel Minister*, p 30.
[40] Gatiss (ed.), *Sermons*, Vol. 1, p 70.
[41] Gatiss (ed.), *Sermons*, Vol. 1, p 71.
[42] Gatiss (ed.), *Sermons*, Vol. 2, pp 336-346.
[43] Gatiss (ed.), *Sermons*, Vol. 2, p 72.

Christian practice the spiritual discipline of meditation as 'a blessed promoter of the divine life.'[44]

3.4.3. George Whitefield and practical pastoral guidance

The sermons of George Whitefield, while rich in evangelical doctrinal content,[45] and abounding in the various aspects of Christian spiritual life and exercise as seen above, are even further suffused with practical pastoral recommendations for how Christians should conduct private and family life and, to an extent, guidance on how their lives in the larger society should be informed. The pastoral dimension of Whitefield's sermons is seen in particular in his diligence to practically work out and apply doctrinal material carefully across the various demographics of listeners present, and this using simple, plain language. As he would comment,

> I speak in plain language; you know my way of preaching. I do not want to play the orator. I do not want to be counted a scholar. I want to speak so as I may reach poor people's hearts.[46]

In line with this aim for simplicity and practicality, Whitefield would give focused sermon applications under categories as follows: 'Now let me address you strangers to Christ;' 'Let me address you ministers of the Gospel;' 'Now it's time to address you busy merchants;' other times, 'Let me address you who are walking with the Lord.' His addresses to these categories above are not formulaic, but show the preacher's particular attention to the practical pastoral dimension of his preaching task – the application of God's word specifically tailored to the needs of his hearers.

Whitefield's sermons directly touched on practical matters of moral concern. A representative instance of this was his sermon, *The Heinous Sin of Drunkenness* preached in 1739. Here he would denounce the 'plague of drinking' that was ravaging English society in particular, show its dire spiritual implications, and offer steps to the believer to overcome its lure.

The problem of alcohol consumption at the period of this sermon was a major social epidemic – dubbed the 'Gin Craze' – that precipitated all kinds of societal ills, not to mention a major spiritual and moral

---

[44] Gatiss (ed.), *Sermons*, Vol. 2, p 72.
[45] For which see Benjamin Dean's chapter in the present volume.
[46] Gatiss (ed.), *Sermons*, Vol. 2, p 395.

crisis.[47] The massive popularity of taverns and gin houses, and the inordinate amounts of time people spent there to the neglect of their daily affairs, made for ills such as desertion of families, mothers abandoning infants, prostitution, general wantonness, and major health challenges.[48] The crisis would defy interventions from diverse sources, including the magistrate's efforts to crack down on bootleggers and close drinking dens. Whitefield in his sermon would comment exasperatedly:

> Some of our civil magistrates have not been slow to use the power given them from above, for the punishment and restraint of such evil doings.... Though their labour, we trust, has not been altogether in vain in the Lord, yet thousands, and I could almost say ten thousands, fall daily at our right-hand, by this sin of drunkenness, in our streets.[49]

George Whitefield's sermon, against the background of this episode, captures not just the content of his pastoral preaching but, importantly, the concern of his preaching to address pressing realities with which his audiences were faced. If the world truly was his parish, as he asserted,[50] Whitefield targeted his sermons to provide spiritual oversight and pastoral guidance in a major crisis to all who would listen. To this crisis of drunkenness he saw his sermon as an attempt at a spiritual remedy, where other means had proved abortive: 'It is high time therefore,' he proclaimed, 'for thy ministers, O God, to lift up their voices like a trumpet, And since human threats cannot prevail, to set before them

---

[47] Whitefield's caption of the situation of the times, 'plague of drinking,' is very accurate. In the first decades of the eighteenth century, there was a major crisis of alcohol abuse in the slums of Georgian London and beyond. The popularization of gin, the newly introduced cheap alcoholic beverage became among the masses a major indulgence and means of entertainment and escapism. One source estimates that in the 1730s about 10 million gallons of gin per year were brewed in London alone and sold from about 7000 dram shops, with an average individual consumption of 14 gallons per year. See, Callum Whittaker, *Private Vice or Public Nuisance: Criticism of Drunkenness in 18th Century Britain* [Web:] http://www.academia.edu/2909107/Private_Vice_or_Public_Nuisance_Criticism_of_Drunkenness_in_18th_Century_Britain [Date of access: 28 Aug. 2015].

[48] Whittaker, *Private Vice or Public Nuisance*. Also, [Web:] http://www.history.co.uk/study-topics/history-of-london/18th-century-gin-craze [Date of access: 28 Aug. 2015].

[49] Gatiss (ed.), *Sermons*, Vol. 2, p 315.

[50] See Boyd Stanley Schlenther, 'Whitefield, George (1714–1770)' in *Oxford Dictionary of National Biography* (Oxford: Oxford University Press, 2004).

the terrors of the Lord and try if these will not persuade them to cease from the evil of their doings.'[51]

Whitefield would go on to warn his listeners against the 'dangers of drunkenness, among which: the impairment of reason, the facilitation of numerous other sins by drunkenness and, the irresponsible living it encouraged. But most importantly for him, he showed the listeners that drunkenness is sin against one's body, defiling the bodily temple and disconnecting the believer from sweet communion with the Holy Spirit.

He would then give recommendations on 'how to conquer the demon drink.' His is both a supernatural and a pragmatic solution. As expected of Whitefield, the first thing needed is an inner transformation of such a life by the power of God. Only God can change the Ethiopian's skin or the leopard's spots.[52] He would encourage his hearers not to despair at the depth of their sin, but to call out to God:

> If you pour out your hearts before him in *daily prayer* and ask assistance from above, it may be that God will endue you with power from on high and make you more than conquerors through Jesus Christ.[53]

Practically, Whitefield would also recommend that people that have an inclination to the bottle should avoid the bad company that would tempt their weaknesses. He would call for 'strict self-denial' and mortification of the flesh vis-à-vis bondage to alcohol, and as a general practice of Christian living.

Whitefield's sermons provide practical pastoral guidance on a host of other topics and life concerns, some of which border on how to maintain good work ethics without neglecting religion; how to listen to sermons profitably;[54] steps to avoid a profane, swearing tongue; raising up children in early piety; and directions on how to keep Christmas, among many others.

3.5. Conclusion

It has been the burden of this article to explore the pastoral dimension of George Whitefield from a select sampling of his written sermons. We

---

[51] Gatiss (ed.), *Sermons*, Vol. 2, p 315.
[52] Gatiss (ed.), *Sermons*, Vol. 2, p 323. An obvious echo of Jeremiah 13:23.
[53] Gatiss (ed.), *Sermons*, Vol. 2, p 323 (emphasis original).
[54] See Adriaan Neele's chapter in the present volume for discussion.

have attempted to paint a portrait of the celebrity evangelist-revivalist whose sermons, though preached on widely different occasions and often focused on conversion, yet are at their core informed and motivated by Whitefield's deeply pastoral heart. It has been presented that the pastoral task of the spiritual nurture of souls, and the cultivation of the Godly life, as 'the one thing needful,' could be seen to serve for Whitefield as the underlying motivation of his sermons. It has been argued that whether preaching on conversion within the context of a large revival meeting, or sharing fellowship with a more intimate gathering of clergy and mature Christians, Whitefield's sermon foci on regeneration, conceived as broadly as he does, are essentially tools of pastoral care and nurturing of the spiritual life. This spiritual life, however, is not circumscribed to matters of religion and practice, but for Whitefield extends to every aspect of the experience of a Christian.

We may conclude, therefore, by returning to our starting questions: That even without preaching in the more settled context of a long-term pastor-congregation relationship, the nature of Whitefield's sermons is deeply pastoral in motivation and delivery. His 'pastoral sermons', therefore, refer not to a particular corpus of sermons reckoned particularly 'pastoral', but to the spirit of his sermons as a whole.

Given the nature of his ministry, the instrument of preaching then became in his hands the chief tool of his caring for God's flock across a wide geographical spread. The sermon thus became for Whitefield, not *merely* episodes of information delivery of biblical and theological content; but as spiritual and practical interventions in the lived experiences of his audience in all their social, intellectual, spiritual, and economic diversities; they were sessions of divine encounter, biblical instruction, as well as occasions of heightened experiences of the Holy Spirit all aimed at the transformation of lives, the inclination of rebellious wills towards God, and the precipitation of decisions to live for God. Whitefield truly demonstrates that in a sense he was properly a pastor, but it was the world that was his parish.

3.6. Sources

The Works of Jonathan Edwards. Vol 4. New Haven: Yale University Press, 1957-2008.

Gatiss, Lee. *The Sermons of George Whitefield*, Volumes 1 & 2. Wheaton, IL: Crossway, 2012.

Kidd, Thomas. *George Whitefield: America's Spiritual Founding Father*. New Haven: Yale University Press, 2014.

Lovejoy, David S. *Religious Enthusiasm and the Great Awakening*. Englewood Cliffs, N.J.: Prentice-Hall, 1969.

Petersen, Randy. *The Printer and the Preacher: Ben Franklin, George Whitefield, and the Surprising Friendship That Invented America*. Nashville, TN.: Thomas Nelson, 2015.

Schlenther, Boyd Stanley. 'Whitefield, George (1714–1770)' in *Oxford Dictionary of National Biography*. Oxford: Oxford University Press, 2004.

Stout, Harry. *The Divine Dramatist: George Whitefield and the Rise of Modern Evangelicalism*. Grand Rapids, MI: Wm. B. Eerdmans, 1991.

Tyerman, L. *The Life of Rev. George Whitefield*, Vol. 1. London: Hodder and Stoughton, 1876.

Whitefield, George. *The Duty of a Gospel Minister*. Glasgow: Robert Shaw, 1741.

Whittaker, Callum. *Private Vice or Public Nuisance: Criticism of Drunkenness in 18th Century Britain*. http://www.academia.edu/2909107/Private_Vice_or_Public_Nuisance_Criticism_of_Drunkenness_in_18th_Century_Britain [Date of access: 28 Aug. 2015].

4. Whitefield's Evangelical Theology
by Benjamin Dean

In an essay celebrating the impact of George Whitefield's ministry, Bishop J. C. Ryle remarked:

> [Whitefield] was a man of extraordinary charity, catholicity, and liberality in his religion. He knew nothing of that narrow-minded feeling which makes some men fancy that everything must be barren outside their camps, and that their own party has got a complete monopoly of truth in heaven. He loved all who loved the Lord Jesus Christ in sincerity.[1]

Whitefield's generous, unifying spirit is a well-attested feature of his persona. Despite disagreements, difficulties and misunderstandings, John Wesley reckoned that firm and faithful friendship was 'the distinguishing part of his character.'[2] In a memorial sermon at the time of Whitefield's death, another prominent minister, who had originally been converted during Whitefield's early career began in a similar vein, declaring:

> Mr Whitefield was no partisan in religion. His spirit was not narrow and contracted, but he cordially embraced all ... true followers of Christ, of every opinion, name and nation, however in circumstantials, modes, and external forms of worship they might differ from him: yet he was zealous, steady and unshaken in the great and fundamental truths of the Gospel.[3]

As early as the year 1739, aged 24, Whitefield had expressed such desire when he wrote: 'I long to see a catholic spirit over-spread the world; may God vouchsafe to make me an instrument in promoting it.'[4] The classical term 'catholicity' means 'universal,' 'embracing all,' and it is historically demonstrable that Whitefield's 'liberality' was responsible for hugely significant growth in interdenominational association and partnership.

---

[1] George Whitefield, *Select Sermons of George Whitefield M.A.: With an Account of His Life by J.C. Ryle and a Summary of His Doctrine by R. Elliot* (London: Banner of Truth Trust, 1959), p 30.
[2] Thomas S. Kidd, *George Whitefield: America's Spiritual Founding Father* (New Haven: Yale University Press, 2014), p 253.
[3] Whitefield, *Select Sermons*, p 35.
[4] Iain Murray, 'George Whitefield and Christian Unity,' in *Heroes* (Edinburgh: Banner of Truth, 2008), p 64.

Whitefield's unique role so effectively promoted a spirit of Christian unity, appealed to its attractiveness, and worked at collaboration so tirelessly that he is justifiably counted the founding father of transatlantic evangelicalism. Following thorough documentation of the historical basis for such a claim, our subject's most recent full-scale and sympathetically critical biographer concludes that,

> Whitefield was the most influential Anglo-American evangelical leader of the eighteenth century. His colleague and rival John Wesley left a greater organizational legacy, and his ally Jonathan Edwards made a more significant theological contribution. But Whitefield was the key figure in the first generation of evangelical Christianity; of the three, he linked, by far, the most pastors and leaders through his relentless travels, preaching, publishing and letter-writing networks. Without him, Anglo-American evangelicalism would have hardly represented a coherent movement. From his first remarkable meetings at Moorfields to his last tour of the colonies, he saw and met more people in Britain, Ireland, and America than any other person of the era. His labors, above any other factor, virtually invented a sense of common transatlantic evangelical identity.[5]

Despite deep theological disagreements and personality clashes with friends and associates of various hues, 'his teaching and example prepared the way for the great era of evangelical cooperation after his death.'[6]

Yet it is crucial to recognize that Whitefield's catholic spirit had definite and particular theological content. Far from being a matter of shallow indifference, loyalty to certain core points of doctrine was for

---

[5] Kidd, *Whitefield*, p 260. On Whitefield's role in the creation of 'tangible links' that grew into networks, see David Ceri Jones, 'Calvinistic Methodism and English Evangelicalism,' in Michael A. G. Haykin and Kenneth J. Stewart (eds.), *The Emergence of Evangelicalism: Exploring Historical Continuities* (Nottingham: Apollos, 2008), pp 112–128. 'By the summer of 1741 ... Whitefield had woven together a Calvinistic evangelical movement; sympathetic evangelicals in England, Wales, Scotland, and the American colonies had been introduced to one another and had begun to dream that perhaps they represented the first intimation of the start of the millennial reign of Christ. It is hard to overestimate the role of [sic] Whitefield's personality and dynamic revivalism played in the creation of this network' (p 115). In this regard consult also Mark A. Noll, *The Rise of Evangelicalism: The Age of Edwards, Whitefield, and the Wesleys* (Downers Grove, Ill.: InterVarsity Press, 2004), pp 96-107.

[6] Murray, 'George Whitefield and Christian Unity,' p 51; cf. Kidd, *Whitefield*, p 153. Differences between the teaching of Whitefield and Wesley on sin, justification, and regeneration are explored in Ian J. Maddock, *Men of One Book. A Comparison of Two Methodist Preachers, John Wesley and George Whitefield* (Cambridge: Lutterworth Press, 2011), pp 176-231.

him completely decisive. Whitefield believed Christian unity was a confessional unity, built around precise adherence to chief teachings. It is a profoundly learned unity revolving around great precepts, 'that all who believe in the fundamental gospel truths, necessary for salvation, are one.'[7] They are those who 'love Jesus Christ in sincerity and truth.'[8] The spiritual awakening (often termed the 'evangelical revival') in which Whitefield was instrumental led to the coining of the term 'evangelical' as a descriptive title precisely to summarize the strong theological accord about the substance of these principal truths.[9]

'[E]ssentials of the gospel' (2:442)[10] are of course held within a broad framework of basic beliefs concerning God and creation – Trinity, Attributes, Election, Providence, and so on.[11] Yet the foremost elements of the Gospel message of salvation, that God saves hell-deserving sinners through regeneration and justification in Christ were, for Whitefield, vital and non-negotiable. These he 'preached and insisted on' from the outset.[12] Because these teachings encapsulate the benefits acquired by Christ's

---

[7] Murray, 'George Whitefield and Christian Unity,' p 51.
[8] Whitefield, *Works*, Vol. 5, pp 130-2; cited in Murray, 'George Whitefield and Christian Unity,' p 48.
[9] See J.I. Packer and Thomas Oden (eds.), *One Faith: The Evangelical Consensus* (Wheaton, IL: Crossway, 2004).
[10] Volume and page references throughout refer to Lee Gattis (ed.), *The Sermons of George Whitefield*. 2 Volumes (Wheaton, IL: Crossway, 2012).
[11] On the super-structure of Christian doctrine as 'the double theme of God and his works,' and the setting of soteriology – not itself the material centre and heart of Christian truth – in a comprehensive account of the works of the Triune God, see John Webster, '*Rector Et Iudex Super Omnia Genera Doctrinarum?* The Place of the Doctrine of Justification,' in Michael Weinrich and John P. Burgess (eds.), *What Is Justification About? Reformed Contributions to an Ecumenical Theme* (Grand Rapids, MI: Eerdmans, 2009), pp 35-56. '[T]he only Christian doctrine that may legitimately claim to exercise a magisterial and judicial role in the corpus of Christian teaching is the doctrine of the Trinity, since in that doctrine alone all other doctrines have their ultimate basis. Other topics of Christian teaching may from time to time become particularly acute points of theological conscience, in which the fidelity of church and theology to the gospel is at stake. Among such topics, teachings about the person and work of Christ have in the course of Christian history had a high profile. But they have played that role, not because they are in and of themselves the sole bearers of Christian truth or because they comprehend all teaching within themselves, but because in them is made especially visible the fact that the triune God is in himself the first and the last' (p 38).
[12] Elliot in Whitefield, Select Sermons, p 35. See further, Michael A.G. Haykin, *The Revived Puritan: The Spirituality of George Whitefield* (Dundas, Ontario: Joshua Press, 2000), pp 40-48. The doctrines of conversion and regeneration were those most at issue in Whitefield's divergence from much Anglican officialdom (Kidd, *Whitefield*, pp 63-64, 122-123).

incarnate person and work, and enunciate the all-important truths and conditions of God's relationship to people in a world of wrath and death, they took for Whitefield precedence over loyalty to any denomination. These, indeed, were the doctrines that gave Whitefield's evangelism its leading edge and drove the revival movement of which he was a spearhead.[13] These we shall describe in some detail.

This did not mean that, for Whitefield, matters of secondary importance – 'non-essentials' (2:443) – were mere opinion. Issues of second-order significance may still have first-order implications. As Whitefield's early exchange with Jonathan Edwards about direct guidance from the Holy Spirit or his long-standing arguments with John Wesley regarding 'free will' and 'universal redemption' demonstrated, disputes about secondary matters are serious because they concern the content of God's revelation in Scripture, and what is therefore to be believed, taught and lived.[14]

A full survey of the character of Whitefield's theology would include themes as fundamental as the authority of Scripture or the incomparable majesty and uniqueness of Jesus Christ.[15] It would have also to consider themes such as unconditional election and final perseverance (the subject of Melvin Tinker's essay). Whitefield's theology in these respects as in others was 'in no way innovative.'[16]

But this is not to suggest that he was an amateur at doctrine. His immediate theological ancestry was Reformed orthodoxy, a moderate Calvinism shaped by the Puritans and Matthew Henry, directly informing his understanding of biblical theology and Christian ministry. His conceptual grasp was clear, competent, exact, firm, rich and sophisticated. It is difficult to find any particular point of teaching where he was definitely wrong (advocacy of slavery excepted, on which see below). Whitefield's special virtue was to present original, apostolic faith, in fresh expression and form, and his sermons show that he did so with intellectual power and weight.

---

[13] Ian J. Shaw, 'Nineteenth Century Perceptions,' in Michael A. G. Haykin and Kenneth J. Stewart (eds.), *The Emergence of Evangelicalism: Exploring Historical Continuities* (Nottingham: Apollos, 2008), p 313.
[14] Murray, 'George Whitefield and Christian Unity,' pp 57-58.
[15] Whitefield's presentation of the person and work of Christ rewards close study. For instance, survey 1:109-122, 215-241, 355-365 and 2:441-456.
[16] J.I. Packer, 'The Spirit with the Word: The Reformation Revivalism of George Whitefield,' in *Honouring the People of God. The Collected Shorter Writings of J.I. Packer*. Volume 4 (Carlisle: Paternoster Press, 1999), p 50.

But that is to understate his style. This sermon-opener serves as a taste of Whitefield's directness:

> I suppose I may take it for granted, that of you, among whom I am now about to preach the kingdom of God, are fully convinced, that it is appointed for all men once to die and that ye all really believe that after death comes the judgment and the consequences of that judgment will be, that ye must be doomed to dwell in the blackness of darkness, or ascend to dwell with the blessed God, forever and ever (1:384).

Here is theology through personality delivered with breath-taking force and verve, verging on aggression. His sermons blend doctrinal clarity with grip, immediacy, and urgency; 'a mixture of spiritual zeal and raw charisma.'[17] The effect is exceptional penetration, impassioned, forthright, and extraordinarily vivid.

My objective in this chapter is to set out the central themes of Whitefield's soteriology, his understanding of salvation. Forgiveness and transformation in Christ by the power of the Holy Spirit are the meat of the matter. But before examining Whitefield's approach to these things it is necessary to appreciate our subject's view of their critical necessity, i.e. their setting against a background of sin and Divine judgment.

4.1. *Original sin*

Whitefield understood original sin as that universal state where every person has a nature inclined toward evil and wields a shocking capacity for perpetrating it. This is the general condition of our existence in corruption – affecting all levels of a fallen, cursed creation. '[E]verything in the world is out of order,' he said, and

> I have often thought ... that if there were no other argument to prove original sin, the rising of wolves and tigers against man, nay, the barking of a dog against us, is a proof of original sin.[18]

In an early sermon 'Walking with God' (1:66-68), Whitefield defined the essence of sin as 'the prevailing power of enmity' in human hearts against God. Such 'heart-enmity' is an ingrained 'averseness,' an inherent hostility and propensity to oppose God (1:67). It is the inclination to resist God and God's law, to put his gifts to perverse use, distorting whatever

---

[17] Noll, *Rise of Evangelicalism*, p 98.
[18] Whitefield, *Select Sermons*, pp 51-52.

knowledge of truth there may be. Man in this condition hides from God, avoids contact or relation with God, evades responsibility to God, neglects duty to God, and rises up in competition against God (1:66). Such 'irreconcilable' hatred of God, with its desperate wickedness, deceit, guilt and misery, has been transmitted since man's first disobedience in Adam through Cain. 'And all that open sin and wickedness, which like a deluge has overflowed the world, are only so many streams running from this dreadful contagious fountain' (1:67). Whitefield's teaching on the transmission of sin is, to the contemporary mind at least, very severe indeed. In 'Marks of a True Conversion' he maintained that children come into the world with the guilt of Adam resting upon them, 'imputed' to them. Far from being innocent, as 'a blank piece of white paper' (1:388), infants, being conceived and born in sin are morally corrupt and therefore culpable. Whitefield thought parents would agree that children display 'self-will and aversion to goodness ... because they bring enmity' to God 'into the world with them.' Children born in the condition of sin are 'children of wrath,' sensual, carnal, prone to misdirection. Infant mortality, he thought, is obvious evidence in the matter, for how could God permit the sickness and death of little children 'unless Adam's first sin' is imputed to them? (1:389).

At this juncture, Whitefield's account combines and (to my mind) confuses the inheritance of a sinful nature with personal condemnation resulting from true moral guilt for sins committed. This distinction requires urgent biblical clarification.[19] For children to be conceived in

---

[19] Note Whitefield's appeal to Anglican Article IX on this issue (2:242) in his sermon 'Justification in Christ' (2:239-249), where he seems to blend of elements of 'federalism' and 'realism.' Henri Blocher, *Original Sin: Illuminating the Riddle* (Leicester: Apollos, 1997), pp 63-83, combines exegetical, historical and systematic work on Romans 5:12-14, offering a range of important corrective remarks. The Augustinian-Reformed tradition, exemplified by Turretin, perceives Adam's federal headship implying imputation of (alien) sin to his descendants: 'before they are conceived, they are condemned,' receiving a polluted nature 'and sentenced to death' (p 65). The main problems with this view of 'inherited guilt' regard its baffling account of personal responsibility and its highly questionable grounding in biblical exegesis. Bearing part of the consequences of Adam's or others' sin on the one hand, and liability to Divine punishment for it on the other, are two distinct themes in Scripture (p 75). Blocher proposes an interpretation as follows: 'it can be said that through the one disobedience of Adam, of which all human sins are offshoots, all have been constituted sinners' (p 78). This, he argues, allows 'the unattested and difficult thesis of imputation of an alien sin [to be] avoided – without downplaying the tragic reality of the Augustinian human predicament' (p 80). For an excellent formulation, companionable to Blocher's, which understands original sin in terms of total depravity whilst rejecting the concept of 'original guilt,' see Oliver Crisp, 'On Original Sin,' *International Journal of Systematic Theology* 17:3. (2015), pp 252-266.

sin, born within the corrupted conditions of a cursed creation and so to inherit a sinful human nature is one thing. To bear personal guilt for the sins of others and/or legal responsibility along with the wicked is another. What kind of God, it may be asked, holds small infants personally culpable, liable, deserving as individuals the ravages of disease, war, or accident ahead of eventual perdition? Is this the teaching of Christ and Scripture?[20]

Mercifully, Whitefield qualifies things somewhat, recognizing the comparative innocence of the 'little children' Jesus spoke about in Matthew 18:3. Children are not totally innocent, yet they are innocent by comparison with adults (1:389). His burden is, though, to impress upon parents the importance of prayerful godliness, baptism, education, instruction and nurture. Otherwise, Whitefield warns, at the final judgment children will inform their parents that, alongside their own wickedness, responsibility for their damnation belongs to poor training in the faith (1:390).[21]

Most significantly, teaching about sin is a point where Whitefield felt that faithful evangelical ministry and a false ministry could readily be distinguished.

> As God can send a nation or a people no greater blessing than to give them sincere and upright ministers, so the greatest curse that God can possibly send upon people in this world, is to give them over to blind, unregenerate, carnal, lukewarm, and unskilful guides.[22]

The counterfeit minister treats the topic of sin lightly, smoothly, superficially, preferring to preach a peace 'of the devils making,' counting the tragedy of spiritual and moral depravity of little consequence. The pattern of true grace, however, that grace which indeed brings genuine

---

[20] For useful discussion of this cluster of issues and a constructive proposal for 'Christological Realism,' refer to Marcus Peter Johnson, *One in Christ. An Evangelical Theology of Salvation* (Wheaton, IL: Crossway, 2013), pp 61-77.

[21] Rather than reserving harshest denunciation for everyone but himself, Whitefield apparently subjected his own conscience to intense scrutiny. Periods of self-examination revealed to him the darkness of his own heart and nature. It seems that at one juncture he found so distressing his unfitness and unworthiness ('actual sins and natural deformity') that he was tempted to retire from the ministry. The deep sense of personal corruption and guilt, however, seems to have brought the miracle of God's grace more fully through to him (Arnold A. Dallimore, *George Whitefield: God's Anointed Servant in the Great Revival of the Eighteeenth Century* (Wheaton, IL: Crossway, 1990), p 68).

[22] Whitefield, *Select Sermons*, p 49.

peace with God, begins by painting in dark colours because of concern for genuine conviction of sin: 'before you can speak peace to hearts, you must be made to see, made to feel, made to weep over, made to bewail, your actual transgressions against the law of God.'[23]

Whitefield believed that people must not merely recognize their sins and feel the wound of them, but sense also God's displeasure toward them in his rejection of their sins. The force and fury of God's anger toward evil must be known inwardly in the heart for true repentance to occur. Such emphasis is characteristic of Whitefield's evangelistic preaching, and underpinned by robust understanding of God's outrage, indignant wrath, and inflexible opposition to the general condition of original sin, and the manner in which God's justice causes a rejection of its appearance in the transgressions of particular people. Whitefield did not prescribe precisely the same pattern and 'pungent' degree of contrition for all persons. But the bitterness, the black dread of our actual sins in light of God's hatred of them, the sheer distress of sensing the threat of Divine judgment against us is indeed evidence of the Holy Spirit's operation and so must in some significant measure precede a soul coming to peace with God.

> [I]f you never felt this inward corruption, if you never saw that God might justly curse you for it, indeed, my dear friends, you may speak to your hearts, but I fear, nay, I know, there is no true peace.[24]

Whitefield's Calvinist convictions ensured appreciation of natural or 'total depravity' – everything in everyone is impacted by and infected with sin – and denied that believers ever reach the point of being beyond temptation. Sinless perfection was, for him, a fantastical notion. Most pernicious of all, Whitefield thought, 'the last idol to be rooted out of the heart,' is self-righteous hypocrisy.[25] And it is here that the offence of his preaching may perhaps be most keenly registered, for Whitefield believed that many, even most, who lived and worked in the fellowship of established church and practice, following its faith and using means of grace were not true Christians, but rather relying on themselves, on their own piety, without Christ in them, at enmity still with God and in reality 'just hanging over hell.'[26] Whitefield assumed such and was convinced that appealing to them was a sign of care.

---

[23] Whitefield, *Select Sermons*, p 50.
[24] Whitefield, *Select Sermons*, p 52.
[25] Whitefield, *Select Sermons*, p 72.
[26] Whitefield, *Select Sermons*, p 57.

Indeed, his strategy in speaking so sharply against falsehood and God's displeasure at it was to provoke true spiritual awareness. To be in hell without Christ, tormented forever together with the devil, Whitefield counted as strong inducement to 'fly for [our] lives to Christ, fly to a bleeding God, fly to a throne of grace.'[27] Officialdom has never counted such rhetoric popular, but against the ever-present perils of formalism, immorality, and heresy, he understood the threat of damnation as in reality an act of genuine love.

4.2. Eternal judgment

As we shall see, Whitefield was convinced that the 'prevailing power of ... enmity' is only disarmed and 'destroyed in every soul that is truly born of God and gradually more and more weakened as the believer grows in grace and the Spirit of God gains a greater and greater ascendency in the heart' (1:68). Moreover, unless people do receive the gift of the Holy Spirit there is no escape from everlasting damnation. Whitefield taught, quite deliberately, 'That the torments reserved for the wicked hereafter, are eternal' (1:442).[28] The 'judgment of hell' (Matthew 23:33) he understood as an entirely real permanent state, consequent upon final refusal of God's gracious claim upon his creatures. Conditional immortality or annihilation is ruled out. Indeed, these were to be consciously opposed as 'Antichristian,' whether espoused by high-ranking Anglicans, rationalist critics or wider popular opinion.[29] Instead, Whitefield's account of hell is as a never-ending, ceaseless state of destruction and banishment, bearing

---

[27] Whitefield, *Select Sermons*, p 58.
[28] 'The Eternity of Hell Torments' (1:441-452).
[29] Kidd, *Whitefield*, pp 54-55, 86-87, 106-107. Regarding Whitefield's alignment with Anglican formularies here, the 'Great Litany' in the *Book of Common Prayer* plainly petitions for deliverance from 'everlasting damnation.' Cranmer's second and third homilies, 'Of the misery of all mankind, and of his condemnation to death everlasting by his own sin' and 'Of salvation ... from sin and death everlasting' are also explicit. Relevant wording within the sermons is: 'damnation, and death everlasting,' 'sinful, wretched, and damnable,' 'captivity of sin, death, and hell,' 'everlasting captivity of the devil and his prison of hell,' 'Christ for our sakes suffered most painful death, to redeem us from everlasting death,' 'saved from everlasting damnation by Christ,' and 'whereas we were condemned to death and hell everlasting ... the intent [of God is] to justify us and restore us to life everlasting' (*Homilies*. London: SPCK, 1938; Orig. 1562; pp 17,19,21,30,31). The most sustained, rigorous, and convincing recent critique of conditionalism is the collection of studies in Christopher W. Morgan and Robert A. Peterson (eds.), *Hell under Fire: Modern Scholarship Reinvents Eternal Punishment* (Grand Rapids, MI: Zondervan, 2004).

the full brunt of God's retributive justice through the infliction of pain in a perpetual conscious experience of Divine punishment in endless time for an unlimited duration.

Rather than being a disproportionate stress in his preaching, Whitefield's convictions about eternal judgment provided the backdrop of his Gospel preaching and a significant motivation for it. Evocation of eternal wrath was for Whitefield the context within which escape and rescue through Christ is best appreciated. He felt obliged to warn avoidance of this most dire destiny.

Whitefield frankly admits the shocking nature of teaching 'that an eternity of misery awaits the wicked in a future state' (1:442). Still, he reckoned that eternal punishment, misery and torment, 'terrors of the Lord,' are the strongest dissuasive from sin and unbelief (1:442). The profoundest meaning of salvation is deliverance from being 'damned forever' (2:447) in the unremitting hell of God's continuing wrath. To warn concerning this outcome and urge people to avoid it, as Christ did and his servants should, is actually merciful and loving.

Whitefield offers several arguments in support of hell as unending torment:

1. Scriptural imagery, concepts, and themes indicate eternal perdition as biblical teaching. Scriptural revelation is the only certain knowledge we have regarding hell, and the 'endless duration' of outer darkness, contempt, unquenchable fire, and an undying worm is, Whitefield believed, clear and evident. 'Ever and ever,' 'understood in a spiritual sense,' means for unlimited 'term of years,' a perpetual succession of time (1:444).

2. The survival and continuance of the human soul in a state either of torture or bliss through the course of two parallel destinies.[30] In biblical usage, warnings of everlasting punishment are counterpart to promises of everlasting life, and though different in every other regard both states share the quality of duration, being by definition unceasing. Threats and promises stand together, beside one another, in the Gospel. Because of our 'weak apprehensions,' reasons Whitefield, God's punishment appears 'far to exceed the crime' (1:445). God is more readily inclined to reward those who respond to

---

[30] For competent initial discussion concerning the metaphysical coherence of this point, to Jerry L. Walls, 'Heaven and Hell,' in Thomas P. Flint and Michael C. Rea (eds.), *The Oxford Handbook of Philosophical Theology* (Oxford: OUP, 2009), pp 491-511.

the Gospel, than he is poised to punish those who refuse to repent. But to deny the reality of 'gospel threatenings' is pure folly (1:446).

3. The nature of the covenant. Jesus Christ is the mediator between God and humanity, as the only Saviour given for deliverance of sinners. The time-span between physical birth and physical death – this current life – is the one and only window of opportunity assigned by God within which we must turn to him. To die in the wickedness of persistent unbelief is to die under the judgment of God and, therefore, to remain under God's judgment as a perpetual and irreversible state.

'For, since there is no possibility of their being delivered out of such a condition but by and through Christ, and since at the hour of death the time of Christ's meditation and intercession is irrecoverably gone, the same reason that may be given why God should punish a sinner that dieth under the guilt of his sins for a single day, will equally hold good why he should continue to punish him for a year, an age, nay all eternity' (1:446).

4. Hell is eternal torment because it is a fate shared with the devil and demons, and their destiny is everlasting punishment. He anchors this proposal in Jesus' statement (Matthew 25:41) that the Son of Man will banish the 'accursed' to eternal fire prepared for Satan and his angels. The justice of Satan's unending punishment is, Whitefield reasons, incontrovertible, and even though the devil's recompense is more severe in terms of degree, it is equivalent in terms of duration. 'For though [the devil] may have sinned against greater light, ... [people] sin against greater mercy' (1:447).[31]

---

[31] Whitefield's case regarding the destiny of unbelievers as shared with that of the devil could be strengthened by exegesis of Revelation 14:11 and 20:10-15. After thorough review of interpretative questions, the conclusion of Gregory Beale is that these passages are 'the Achilles heel of the annihilationist perspective ... the likelihood is that John believed in an endless judgement of the ungodly' (Gregory K. Beale, 'The Revelation on Hell,' in Christopher W. Morgan and Robert A. Peterson (eds.), *Hell under Fire: Modern Scholarship Reinvents Eternal Punishment* (Grand Rapids, MI: Zondervan, 2004), p 134. A *locus classicus* on this matter from the same period is Jonathan Edwards, 'The Justice of God in the Damnation of Sinners,' in M.X. Lesser (ed.), *The Works of Jonathan Edwards. Volume 19. Sermons and Discourses 1734-1738* (New Haven and London: Yale University Press, 2001), pp 336-376. Edwards' argument therein regarding the fullness and depth of evil deserving everlasting damnation appears more convincing that his reasoning about the comparable 'infinite' quality of all particular sins. An interesting case for degrees of punishment in hell is John Frame, *Systematic Theology: An Introduction to Christian Belief* (Philipsburg, NJ: P&R, 2013), p 1083.

'These thoughts are too melancholy for me to dwell on' Whitefield continues, 'as well as for you to hear. ... But if the bare mentioning of the torments of the damned is so shocking, how terrible must the enduring of them be' (1:451). The terror is supposed to be very great, he maintained, and the disproportion between transitory pleasures of sin now and endless experience of punishment then so striking that escaping God's eternal judgment through repentant trust in Christ is most intelligent counsel.

4.3. *Justification by faith: forgiveness and acceptance*

With sin, guilt, bondage, helplessness and the prospect of ceaseless hell the situation faced by fallen humanity, the distinctive and leading edge of Whitefield's Gospel preaching is an incisive and robust doctrine of justification by faith, with imputation as its conceptual centrepiece.[32] 'Never was there a reformation brought about in the church,' Whitefield declared, 'but by preaching the doctrine of an imputed righteousness.'[33] Justification through imputation concerns how God's righteousness is given in Christ. Christ's whole, moral, personal character and righteousness is counted ours for the purpose of Divine judgment.

This is a vicarious righteousness, a righteousness that stoops and condescends, primarily through atoning for sin. More specifically, Whitefield taught penal substitutionary atonement as the moral condition for justification by God. In the state of sin, humanity cannot bear the consequences, namely:

1. God's punishment and penalty for disobedience (originally communicated to Adam and Eve in their exclusion, pain and death).
2. The requirement that God's justice is served only by reparation for wrongs done.
3. Condemned, alienated, and corrupted, people are utterly unable to live as they ought.

Christ's essential work on our behalf is then twofold: his whole life of active obedience that perfectly fulfils human responsibility to keep God's moral law, and his passive obedience through an ignominious

---

[32] Whitefield, *Select Sermons*, pp 63; 72-84.
[33] Whitefield, *Select Sermons*, p 75; cf. 1:266.

death bearing the curse, punishment and suffering deserved in the face of God's wrath:

> Here then opens the amazing scene of divine philanthropy; I mean, God's love to man: for, behold, what man could not do, Jesus Christ, the Son of his Father's love, undertakes to do for him. ... [H]e obeyed, and thereby fulfilled the whole moral law in our stead; and also died a painful death upon the cross, and thereby became a curse for, or instead of, those whom the Father had given to him.[34]

The Gospel, according to Whitefield, revolves around and entirely hangs upon this atoning righteousness of Christ. The Son, 'being God and man in one person,' through obedience unto death is a satisfaction which 'wrought out a full, perfect, sufficient righteousness for all to whom it was to be imputed.'[35] The blood-sacrifice of Christ's cross ultimately displays God's righteousness and justice by turning God's condemnation away from us.

Grounding justification in penal atonement, that Jesus suffered the wrath of God instead of us, Whitefield is no theological primitive, but a 'spokesman of historic, orthodox Christianity.'[36] His interpretation of the meaning of Christ's death – i.e., how it works in relation to the salvation of humanity – is in formal terms this: 'the same sacrifice that cancels sin by the sacrifice that God has ordained also turns aside his own judicial wrath.'[37] The law is fulfilled and forgiveness for law breaking accomplished. And with forgiveness we come directly to justification, 'that great and fundamental article of our faith' (2:239), and the wellspring of Whitefield's evangelistic preaching.

Justification is a juridical and forensic term (i.e. from the law-court). It means 'being so acquitted in the sight of God as to be looked upon as though we had never offended him at all' (2:241). Pardon, acquittal, the removal of condemnation (for sins past, present and future), full acceptance, legal righteousness and relational peace are ours, who become in Christ 'the righteousness of God.' To be justified by faith

---

[34] Whitefield, *Select Sermons*, p 74; also 1:265. For expansion, cf. the section in 'Justified by his Blood' (2:46-249).
[35] Whitefield, *Select Sermons*, p 74.
[36] Hughes Oliphant Old, *The Reading and Preaching of the Scriptures in the Worship of the Christian Church. Volume 5. Modernism, Pietism, and Awakening* (Grand Rapids, MI: Eerdmans, 2005), p 151.
[37] D.A. Carson, 'Editorial,' *Themelios* 39.1. (2014), p 1. In simpler language, people deserve to be punished for their sin, but Christ (a willing victim of infinite worth) was punished instead, as a substitute, that they may be forgiven.

means present deliverance from the accrued guilt of our corrupt nature, immediate release from the legal consequence of sin in our lives (2:247), and a position clear and right before the law of God. This is a gift received by faith that despairs at self and places confidence exclusively in Christ's person, work and promises.

The imputed righteousness of Christ is here the foundation of forgiveness and acceptance, and Whitefield addressed various misunderstandings about imputation, particularly regarding moral life and responsibility.[38] For example, 'Does Christ's righteousness for us encourage moral irresponsibility from us?' Indeed not. Christ's good works, his thorough fulfilment of God's law is reckoned to us. Our subsequent 'good works' demonstrate that Christ's have been counted to us; they are the 'declarative evidence of our justification.'[39] Godliness is the fruit and result of justification. The life of faith and obedience, with its patterns of moral virtue and excellence, is not pursued in the hope of earning God's forgiveness or attaining acceptance at the last day. 'Works! works!,' Whitefield announced, 'a man get to heaven by works! I would as soon think of climbing to the moon on a rope of sand!'[40] Devoted discipleship to Christ, however impressive, does not secure salvation. Rather, it flows from it as the proof and assurance that salvation is actually received, the ultimate verdict of everlasting innocence and acceptance already passed: 'Some talk of being justified at the day of judgment. That is nonsense. If we are not justified here, we shall not be justified there' (2:452).

4.3.1. *Justification by imputation: the grounds of a fundamental doctrine*

It is sometimes argued that imputation is an incoherent concept. As far as classic Protestant analysis is concerned, this is simply not so. Paul

---

[38] 1:266-272. Exegetical warrant for imputation is discussed and evaluated in the seminal exchange between Robert A. Gundry and D.A. Carson in Mark Husbands and Daniel J. Treier (eds.), *Justification. What's at Stake in the Current Debate?* (Downer's Grove, IL: IVP, 2004), pp 17-78. A thorough and illuminating account of double imputation in the patristic period, establishing its substantial congruence with mainline Reformed dogmatics, is Nick Needham, 'Justification in the Early Church Fathers,' in B.L. McCormack (ed.), *Justification in Perspective: Historical Developments and Contemporary Challenges* (Grand Rapids, MI: Baker Academic, 2006), pp 32-37.

[39] Whitefield, *Select Sermons*, p 75.

[40] Murray, 'George Whitefield and Christian Unity,' p 55; excerpted from Whitefield's sermon, 'Examine yourselves, whether ye be in the faith.'

Helm supplies one of the clearest explanations of what it means to be 'accounted righteous':

> On the Reformed view, Christ's imputed righteousness is 'alien,' external, the righteousness of another, and even when imputed, it will always remain alien. God justifies the ungodly as ungodly. The widely-used illustration, that Christ's righteousness is credited to my account, is misleading. (If I'm credited, mustn't Christ be debited?) To repeat, in the imputation of righteousness, nothing moves. Imputation is not an electronic moral transfer. Righteousness is not transmitted, transfused, or relocated in any way. (Any more than if I receive free insurance cover I receive a transfusion of some mysterious substance called 'insurance.') The believer's imputed righteousness remains inalienably Christ's perfect righteousness. What is true is that by an act of the unspeakable mercy of God the believer is shielded by, or seen through, or covered by, the righteousness of another.[41]

In this regard, Whitefield followed the main lines of Reformation (and Anglican) understanding.

4.3.1.1. *Luther*

Luther scholarship debates the role that imputation plays in his understanding of justification. That it is there is indisputable. See, for instance, the opening synopsis of *Lectures on Galatians*: 'this most excellent righteousness, the righteousness of faith, which God imputes to us through Christ without works ... is a merely passive righteousness'.[42]

The Finnish school locates imputation within the broader theme of union with Christ, such that God's righteousness is not merely ascribed to believers but that Christ's righteousness is really (ontologically) present in believers because of the union. The perceived strength of

---

[41] 'Wright and the Reformation,' http://paulhelmsdeep.blogspot.com/2009/10/wright-and-reformation_3823.html. Accessed 14.06.2015. On the systematic intelligibility of imputation, see Michael Horton, *Covenant and Salvation: Union with Christ* (Louisville: Westminster John Knox, 2007), pp 114-122. In regards to biblical theology, it is correct to position imputation within teaching about incorporation into and union with Christ (so Michael F. Bird, *Evangelical Theology. A Biblical and Systematic Introduction* (Grand Rapids, MI: Zondervan, 2013), pp 562-563), as long as the Scriptural grounds for imputation are given due cognizance (à la Carson's contribution footnote 44 below).

[42] *Lectures on Galatians, 1535, Chapters 1-4. Luther's Works.* Jaroslav Pelikan (ed.) (Saint Louis, MS: Concordia, 1963), p 4.

interpreting imputation as a Divine act that introduces participation in Christ's righteousness through actual indwelling, and thereby as more than a synthetic/legal judgment, is that it launches moral transformation.[43] The probable weakness is an overlapping of justification by imputation (whereby the believer's legal condition is judged through Christ's righteousness) and sanctification (whereby Christ's indwelling righteousness produces actual progress in personal holiness). According to long-established interpretation, Luther's deployment of *reputare* 'pressed the conventional language into the service of a more explicitly status-oriented theology than the previous [medieval Occamist] tradition and paved the way for imputation, rather than impartation, to be the basis of Lutheran understandings of justification'.[44]

4.3.1.2. Anglican doctrine

Anglican Article 11 sets out the doctrine of justification by imputation as the moral linchpin of soteriology: 'We are accounted [*reputamur*] righteous before God only for the merit of our Lord and Saviour Jesus Christ'; (*reputare* is imputation language, being a Latin (Vulgate) rendering of the Greek verb *logizomai*, 'to reckon or impute,' used multiple times in Romans 4:3-12, 22-24, plus Galatians 3:6 and James 2:23).

Cranmer's full-grown conviction about justification is articulated in his three sermons of 1547 (*Homilies*, pp 20-62), and it has been shown that he believed in God's imputation of Christ's righteousness as early as 1538.[45] Forensic imputation is implicitly assumed regarding the communication of Christ's merit in Cranmer's third Homily, 'Of the Salvation of All Mankind.' Deliverance from everlasting death is by 'righteousness of justification, to be received at God's own hands ... the

---

[43] Notger Slenczka, 'Luther's Anthropology,' in Robert Kolb, Irene Dingel, and L'Ubomir Batka (eds.), *The Oxford Handbook of Martin Luther's Theology* (Oxford: Oxford University Press, 2014), p 220; cf. pp 176-7, 265, 268-9, 271 of the same volume for further comment on Luther's forensic and imputative doctrine of justification).

[44] Carl Trueman, '*Simul Peccator Et Justus*: Martin Luther and Justification,' in Bruce L. McCormack (ed.), *Justification in Perspective* (Grand Rapids, MI: Baker, 2006), p 87.

[45] Ashley Null, *Thomas Cranmer's Doctrine of Repentance* (Cambridge: Cambridge University Press, 2000), pp 24, 129-133, 152, 158, 176-178, 215.

forgiveness of sins ... and Christ's merits'.[46] The point is that imputation further clarifies and strengthens the link between Christ's righteousness and the believer's faith, i.e. that it is gratuitous from God's side.

Bullinger's deployment of imputation expresses an additional development in this trajectory of official Reformation Anglican teaching. See, for example, 'The Sixth Sermon' of the *First Decade* in *The Decades of Henry Bullinger*,[47] and 'The First Sermon' in *The Fourth Decade*.[48]

4.3.2. Whitefield and justification by imputation

Like Luther, Calvin[49] and Cranmer before him, Whitefield viewed justification by imputation as essential Protestant doctrine and of capital importance in Christian teaching. This was because he believed that 'imputed righteousness' is in itself immediately decisive for an individual's eternal salvation.[50] In *The Smalcald Articles* (1537), Luther announced with characteristic drama:

Nothing in this article [justification by faith in Christ] can be given

---

[46] *Homilies*, p 20; cf. pp 25, 29. For exposition, see Null, *Thomas Cranmer's Doctrine of Repentance*, pp 215-217, 222, 251-252.

[47] *The Decades of Henry Bullinger*, ed. Thomas Harding (Cambridge: Cambridge University Press, 1849; Orig. 1587), pp 106, 116 (also p 165).

[48] *The Fourth Decade* (Cambridge, 1851), pp 46-48.

[49] Calvin's major treatment is *Institutes*, 3.11-14. On 'imputed righteousness' in early Lutheranism, Calvin, and Protestant orthodoxy, consult Alister McGrath, *Iustitia Dei. A History of the Christian Doctrine of Justification*, 3rd ed. (Cambridge: Cambridge University Press, 2005), pp 238-241, 246 and 270-271.

[50] 'Come, thou doubting creature, who art afraid thou wilt never get comfort. Arise, take comfort, the Lord Jesus Christ, the Lord of life, the Lord of glory, calls for thee. Through his righteousness there is hope for the chief of sinners, for the worst of creatures. ... O let not one poor soul stand at a distance from the Saviour ... O come, come. Now, since it is brought into the world by Christ, so in the name, in the strength and by the assistance of the great God, I bring it now to the pulpit; I now offer this righteousness, this free, this imputed, this everlasting righteousness to all poor sinners who will accept of it ... Think, I pray you, therefore, on these things. Go home, go home, pray over the text and say, "Lord God, thou hast brought an everlasting righteousness into the world by the Lord Jesus Christ. By the blessed Spirit bring it into my heart!" Then die when ye will, ye are safe. If it be tomorrow, ye shall be immediately translated into the presence of the everlasting God – that will be sweet! Happy they who have got this robe on. Happy they that can say, "My God hath loved me and I shall be loved by him with an everlasting love!" That every one of you may be able to say so, may God grant, for the sake of Jesus Christ, the dear Redeemer, to whom be glory forever. Amen' (1:295-296).

up or compromised, even if heaven and earth and things temporal should be destroyed. ... On this article rests all that we teach and practice against the pope, the devil, and the world. Therefore we must be quite certain and have no doubts about it. Otherwise all is lost, and the pope, the devil, and all our adversaries will gain the victory.[51]

Whitefield's agreement on this matter was entire and uncompromising, because he understood justification to concern God's absolute, categorical declaration regarding a person's eternal destiny. 'For the sake of Christ's righteousness alone,' he said,

and not for anything wrought in us, doth God look favourably upon us; we must therefore look for a righteousness without us, even the righteousness of our Lord Jesus Christ. Whoever teaches any other doctrine does not preach the truth as it is in Jesus.[52]

4.4. *Regeneration: the new birth*

Justification regards real legal-positional change before God. Regeneration regards real personal and spiritual transformation before God. If justification is, for Whitefield, the moral basis of Gospel theology a teaching of massive prominence, regeneration is the foremost theme of his evangelistic ministry. Whitefield's preaching of the new birth (from 1732) preceded by a couple of years his proper grasp of justification, and much of the scandal in Anglican officialdom surrounding Whitefield's early career was provoked by his conviction that new birth is necessary for many persons previously baptized.[53] Regeneration, in Whitefield's estimate, is the huge hinge on which Christian teaching hangs, yet something regularly misunderstood.

Physical death entered the world as the penalty for sin and the signal that we have already died spiritually. We need fresh life from Christ through the renewal of a person's inner spirit, a reconstruction of 'the inmost faculties of the mind' and heart (2:275). It is an event so dramatic and profound that the very structure and substance of the self is altered, becoming a 'new creature' through baptism of the

---

[51] Part II; Article I. Theodore G. Tappert, *The Book of Concord: The Confessions of the Evangelical Lutheran Church* (Philadelphia: Fortress Press, 2000; Orig. 1959), p 292.
[52] Whitefield, *Select Sermons*, p 37.
[53] Kidd, *Whitefield*, pp 63-64, 122-123.

Holy Spirit (2:276). The Spirit's operation here brings a person's being into union with Jesus Christ. Regeneration means

> inward change and purity of heart and cohabitation of his Spirit. To be in [Christ], so as to be mystically united to him by a true and lively faith and thereby to receive spiritual virtue from him ... [a] baptism ... of the heart, in the Spirit (2:277).

Through new birth the Holy Spirit joins us to Christ and thereby renovates our nature. The result is a change in the quality and temper of the mind, a reordering of inner personhood, such that 'our souls ... are so purged, purified and cleansed from their natural dross, filth, and leprosy ... that they may be properly said to be made new' (2:278). Outward profession and practice alone cannot, of course, come close to achieving this. To effect new life and being in Christ is a sovereign work of God power.

Of the necessity for a new birth and its Scriptural grounding, Whitefield was convinced. But he was aware that because of our estranged nature and its misunderstanding there is widespread ignorance about it. In his sermons, therefore, Whitefield begins by laying out biblical teaching around three main heads.

First, the Old Testament anticipated an ultimate work of God to overhaul the minds, hearts and spirits of his people. Second, the teaching of Christ – the 'great Prophet and instructor of the world' (2:279) – recorded in John 3 that entrance into God's Kingdom rests on an additional birth by the Spirit. Third, the apostle Paul's remark (Titus 3:5) that salvation comes to individuals through 'the washing of regeneration and renewal of the Holy Ghost,' Whitefield took as equivalent to laying aside the old nature and taking on the new, through which we become 'new creatures' (2:279).

A further reason for rebirth is 'the present corrupt and polluted state of man' by comparison with God's 'infinite sanctity,' i.e. God's transcendent holiness (2:280). The difference and distance between God's burning moral purity and mankind's corruption and filth is infinite, such that communion between God and sinful humanity without regeneration is impossible and unthinkable.

In addition, 'the nature of happiness God has prepared for those who unfeignedly love him,' the inheritance of heaven, would be 'vain and presumptuous,' beyond the bounds of possibility for human beings to share in under the condition and influence of sin. Sin so disorders our desires, and loads us with such degrees of sensuality and selfishness that 'total renovation of our depraved natures,' their whole scale replacement, is 'absolute necessity' (2:281) for fitness to the heavenly Kingdom. That we might enjoy the 'happiness our Saviour has purchased by his precious blood' all inclinations, expectations, and dispositions must be purged and recast in the image of Jesus Christ (2:282).

Outward conformity to religious duty or attainment of moral virtue, 'without experiencing a thorough, real, inward change of heart' (2:284), is empty, naked posturing in the face of God's judgment. Felt knowledge of the Spirit's presence through forgiveness, peace and sweetness of joy – the over-all sense of well-being within God's blessing – are founded on the reality of becoming a 'new creature.' New birth makes us children of God and 'open[s] to us an everlasting scene of happiness and comfort ... an eternal succession of pleasures,' possessing a share in the eternal Kingdom (2:287).

Because spiritual rebirth is an 'invisible' operation of the Spirit, occurring beneath the level of consciousness, Whitefield believed that it may not be detected immediately and straightforwardly (2:278). But marks of regeneration do over time become increasingly apparent. Growth in 'spiritual-mindedness,' 'loose to the world,' no longer principally moved by lust and ambition (1:391), 'sensible of our weakness,' aware of dependence, ignorance and inward corruption, 'real Christians will give up their heart, their understandings, their wills, their affections, to be guided by the word, providence and the Spirit of the Lord' (1:392).

Extending the metaphor of new birth, Whitefield recognized the reality of growth in godliness being a serious process over time. 'Young Christians,' he once remarked, 'are like rivulets. ... shallow, yet [they] make great noise. But an old Christian, he makes not much noise, he goes on sweetly like a deep river sliding into the ocean' (1:393).

Those born again, though imperfect, show signs and signals of innocence, harmlessness, honesty, and goodwill to others (1:394). They manifest humility, hunger to learn, the desire for obedience and service, a sense of utter dependence upon God, and gratitude to him. Always child-like in relation to God, the re-born believer should gradually mature, grow and obviously progress (1:396-397). Such development in Christlikeness occurs through the course of 'great trials,' and the heavenly Father sends afflictions and difficulty to discipline his children. Yet comfort is coming, and God's children may live in hope of that.

In his sermon 'Marks of Having Received the Holy Ghost' (2:187-199), Whitefield lays out evidence of rebirth as follows:

1. A concern for prayer. The Spirit's presence moves one to cry to God, seeking forgiveness, help, guidance and grace for one's self and others (2:190-191).

2. A hatred of sin. Not that the born again do not fall into sin, but the overall pattern of tendencies shift and the general direction of habits change. So also their experience of sin alters, causing sorrow and repentance before God (2:191-192).

3. A person who has received the Spirit lives in the world, but not for it. Amid the business of worldly life, her mind is set on heaven and attracted to spiritual concerns and happiness or fulfillment sought such that the world and its allures are overcome (2:192-193).

4. People with the Spirit are marked by love. Fellow believers are loved not in mere affection, but 'because of their relation to God. ... [F]or the grace we see in them and because they love our Lord Jesus in sincerity.' Christian love loves other believers out of love for Christ. Such love among Christian people, Whitefield says further, 'is not confined to any particular set of men,' feels bigotry and party spirit distasteful, 'but is impartial and catholic, a love that embraces God's image wherever it beholds it and that delights in nothing so much as to see Christ's kingdom come' (2:194).

5. Fifthly and finally, those regenerated by the Spirit and character of Jesus Christ understand the necessity of real love for enemies. 'This is,' Whitefield admits, 'a difficult duty to the natural man. But whoever is made partaker of the promise of the Spirit, will find it practicable and easy. For if we are born again of God, we must be like him and consequently delight to be perfect in this duty of doing good to our worst enemies in the same manner, though not in the same degree as he is perfect' (2:395).

Whitefield thought that the presence of such realities in the lives of believers was more certain evidence of genuine renewal than the appearance of an angel from heaven to declare the forgiveness of sins (2:396).

We should observe (in closing) how Whitefield's understanding of justification and regeneration, carrying together the forensic and transformative dimensions of salvation, holds within it the whole of Christian life and destiny. They are but the beginning of the believers' happiness. The righteousness of God for us in justification brings with it the righteousness of God for us in sanctification. Whitefield places this discussion under the heading of holiness. Justification is the cause of sanctification, and sanctification the effect of acceptance and peace with God. If regeneration is the implantation of the new nature, spirit and self, sanctification involves the operation of God's Spirit in shaping soul, understanding, will, affections, memory, conscience and bodily life in a person so that their changed identity as new creatures is substantially realized in lived experienced. In sanctification, 'the total renovation of the whole man,' the grace of Christ 'is copied and transcribed into their souls,' such that growth away from the tendencies of the sinful nature with its darkened corruption, impulses and habits and toward Christlikeness as he becomes progressively formed within them. Believers share thus in the Divine nature. The inward holiness of the Christian is a Triune work, for as temples of the Holy Spirit, 'the whole Trinity dwells and walks in them,' they sit together with Christ in union with him, 'they talk, they walk with him, as a man talketh and walketh with his friend,' the Spirit bears fruit in them, and communion with the Father's love and companionship ever 'flows into their souls,' remaining a permanent feature of the believer's existence.[54]

But even if decisive and permanent, sanctification remains incomplete for the time being, to be fulfilled and perfected hereafter. Sanctification eventually culminates through perseverance in glorification, which moves forward God's work of salvation to its promised end. Again, glorification is rooted in justification because with forgiveness of sins and acquittal the declarative acceptance of justification entails 'a federal right to all good things to come.' The 'privileges' of salvation, from election through adoption into God's family, perseverance and glorification are bound up together. As the obedience of Christ is imputed to believers, Christ's exaltation is reckoned to them as well. His holiness tasted now is but a foretaste of complete liberation in the new creation. There, wickedness and evil cannot trouble or threaten. Entirely free from anxiety and stress, rest and bliss – 'the full enjoyment of all good' – will accompany 'perfect communion' with God among the saints.[55] Felt certainty about inclusion in the new creation gave grip and drive to Whitefield's announcement of the new birth and urgency in his hearers' response to it.[56]

---

[54] Whitefield, *Select Sermons*, pp 64-65.
[55] Whitefield, *Select Sermons*, p 67.
[56] Kidd, *Whitefield*, pp 40, 47-48, 131-132.

4.5. Conclusion

Whitefield once said, 'My one design is to bring poor souls to Jesus Christ.'[57] Justification and regeneration in combination was a two-pronged advance to prosecute that campaign. The motivation driving Whitefield's evangelism and wider ministry – 13 trips by sailboat across the Atlantic Ocean and constant travel whether in the United Kingdom or America, placing his life and safety at constant risk – was supplied by these teachings. Forgiveness and eternal life to lost sinners through the living Lord Jesus, was the sum and substance of Whitefield's evangelical theology. It was the gist of his understanding of the Gospel message. Integral to the one, holy, catholic and apostolic faith, these were the doctrines that stimulated and sustained revival of epic proportions. These teachings are world-changing because they are life-transforming.[58] Let it be hoped that a recovery of understanding about them and confidence in them will spark a great awakening throughout this country and continent in our time.

As a parting moral, here are words from an oration given at the time of Whitefield's funeral:

> If we have been hearers of Mr. Whitefield, and loved him for Christ's sakes and the Gospel, we should strive to make it manifest by continuing to hold fast those precious truths which we have heard from him ... contending earnestly for them against all opposers as he himself did: not because they were his doctrines, but the doctrine of God and of Christ, of all the holy prophets and apostles, as the Scriptures abundantly testify.[59]

4.6. Afterword: Whitefield and slavery

Given this Symposium's location in postcolonial South Africa and Africa, it is particularly appropriate to register that our subject's complicity in and even advocacy of 'humane' chattel slavery remains reprehensible and problematic. Kidd's assessment is unflinching:

> Whitefield contributed to evangelical Christians' troubling record on race relations and ethnic inequality. Whitefield was one of the

---

[57] Tyerman, *Whitefield* 1:433; cited in Noll, *Rise of Evangelicalism*, p 97.
[58] See 'Afterword' below.
[59] Elliot 1959:41.

earliest Anglo-Americans to make serious efforts to reach African Americans ... with the gospel, yet he did not see all that his gospel required of him in the temporal realm. ... Whitefield not only agitated for the introduction of slavery, but also permitted the presence of slaves at Bethesda before they were legal. He did not even liberate Bethesda's slaves at his death.[60]

There is a clearly contradictory feature here: whilst Whitefield did more (probably) than any other to introduce faith in Christ to African American slaves, publicly defended their full humanity, provided 'the first journalistic statement on the subject of slavery' (Stout), and censured abuse among slave owners, when it came to his own orphanage project at Bethesda he took the path of economic and practical expediency. He 'envisioned a kind of benevolent Christian slave-owning, in which masters would educate slaves in the gospel'.[61]

Noll's remarks are similarly telling and worthy of lengthy citation:

Whitefield's all-or-nothing commitment to evangelism at the expense of well-considered Christian social ethics left an ambiguous legacy ... His stance toward institutional slavery is one example. During 1740, he criticised southern slave-owners for mistreating slaves and took special pains on several occasions to preach to slaves. But he also decided on the spur of the moment that, since Europeans were unable or unwilling to work the land supporting his orphanage, it would be 'impracticable' to survive in Georgia without purchasing "a few Negroes" as slaves. Whitefield, who preached so willingly to slaves, hardly gave a thought when he became a slave-owner himself. Much of what Whitefield did was admirable by any standard, and his commitment to Christ-centred preaching was a shining beacon. But while his character and purpose possessed great integrity, there was no consistency to his broader actions, no depth to his thinking about culture. Ready-fire-aim was his style. In a word, much that would be best and much that would be worst in the later history of evangelicals in America was anticipated by Whitefield in this one stirring year.[62]

On the other hand, a related note of ambivalence:

Whitefield was ... an effective preacher to slaves in his many

---

[60] Kidd, *Whitefield*, pp 261-262.
[61] Kidd, *Whitefield*, p 115.
[62] Noll, *Rise of Evangelicalism*, pp 100-101.

journeys to Georgia, South Carolina, and elsewhere in the colonies. ... Whitefield at first attacked the slave system, but then eventually came to accept it and own slaves himself. None the less, his preaching continued to resemble the Wesleys' by addressing black men and women as spiritual equals and by encouraging the formation of informal Methodist societies on plantations. His encouragement of open emotional responses to his messages, no less than his subordination of social distinctions to the imperatives of preaching, likewise made him an effective stimulus of African-American faith.[63]

Moreover, the message of regeneration in Christ that Whitefield (and others) promoted before long undermined and subverted slavery, contributing considerable influence toward its abolishment in North American and Europe.[64] Part of the issue here is correctly appreciating the role of Jesus Christ as world revolutionary. The historian, Will Durant:

> Jesus does not seem to have thought of ending poverty ... He takes for granted, like all ancients, that a slave's duty is to serve his master well ... He is not concerned to attack existing economic or political institutions; on the contrary, he condemns those ardent souls who would "take the Kingdom of Heaven by storm." The revolution he sought was a far deeper one, without which reforms could only be superficial and transitory. If he could cleanse the human heart of selfish desire, cruelty and lust, utopia would come of itself, and all those institutions that rise out of human greed and violence, and the consequent need for law, would disappear. Since this would be the profoundest of all revolutions, beside which all others would be mere coups d'état of class ousting class and exploiting in its turn, Christ was in this spiritual sense the greatest revolutionist in history.[65]

The point is that social problems are spiritually rooted, and there is therefore a theological primacy to evangelism in relation to Christian social action. William Wilberforce himself, for instance, understood

---

[63] Noll, Rise of Evangelicalism, pp 163-4.
[64] For a recent account of this moral revolution, refer to Ian J. Shaw, *Churches, Revolutions & Empires. 1789-1914* (Fearn: Christian Focus, 2012), pp 131-164.
[65] Will Durant, *The Story of Civilization. Part 3. Caesar and Christ. A History of Roman Civilization and of Christianity from Their Beginnings to A.D. 325* (New York, NY: Simon & Schuster, 1944), p 566.

conversion to be the more pressing need, with social transformation being an entailment or consequence of spiritual change. To be sure, there is in a strong link between evangelism and vigorous compassionate concern for social, political, and economic justice. Indeed, persuasive proclamation regarding the Kingdom of God through the Lordship of Jesus Christ is well served by social action. But evangelism retains logical priority because it concerns *eternal* destiny.[66]

4.7. Sources

Beale, Gregory K. "The Revelation on Hell." In *Hell under Fire: Modern Scholarship Reinvents Eternal Punishment*, edited by Christopher W. Morgan and Robert A. Peterson, pp 111-134. Grand Rapids, MI: Zondervan, 2004.

Bird, Michael F. *Evangelical Theology. A Biblical and Systematic Introduction.* Grand Rapids, MI: Zondervan, 2013.

Blocher, Henri. *Original Sin: Illuminating the Riddle.* Leicester: Apollos, 1997.

Burns, Sherard. "Trusting the Theology of a Slave Owner." In *A God-Entranced Vision of All Things: The Legacy of Jonathan Edwards*, edited by John Piper, Justin Taylor and Stephen J. Nichols, 145-171. Wheaton, IL: Crossway Books, 2004.

Carson, D. A. 'Editorial.' *Themelios* 39.1 (2014).

Crisp, Oliver. 'On Original Sin.' *International Journal of Systematic Theology* 17:3 (2015): 252-266.

Dallimore, Arnold A. *George Whitefield: God's Anointed Servant in the Great Revival of the Eighteenth Century.* Wheaton, IL: Crossway, 1990.

Durant, Will. *The Story of Civilization. Part 3. Caesar and Christ. A History of Roman Civilization and of Christianity from Their Beginnings to A.D. 325.* New York, NY: Simon & Schuster, 1944.

Edwards, Jonathan. "The Justice of God in the Damnation of Sinners." In *The Works of Jonathan Edwards. Volume 19. Sermons and Discourses 1734-1738*, edited by M. X. Lesser, 336-376. New Haven and London: Yale University Press, 2001.

---

[66] Melvin Tinker gives a straightforward discussion along these lines [Melvin Tinker, *Salt, Light, and Cities on Hills: Evangelism and Social Action. How Do They Relate to Each Other?* (Darlington: Evangelical Press, 2014), especially pp 38-40, 72, and 90]; cogent critical reflections from an African American author about the mentality that sanctioned slave owning within the 'Christian' cultural ethics of Whitefield's day are presented by Sherard Burns [Sherard Burns, 'Trusting the Theology of a Slave Owner,' in John Piper, Justin Taylor, and Stephen J. Nichols (eds.), *A God-Entranced Vision of All Things: The Legacy of Jonathan Edwards* (Wheaton, IL: Crossway Books, 2004), pp 145-171].

Frame, John. *Systematic Theology: An Introduction to Christian Belief.* Philipsburg, NJ: P&R, 2013.

Gattis, Lee, ed. *The Sermons of George Whitefield.* 2 Volumes. Wheaton, IL: Crossway, 2012.

Haykin, Michael A. G. *The Revived Puritan: The Spirituality of George Whitefield.* Dundas, Ontario: Joshua Press, 2000.

Horton, Michael. *Covenant and Salvation: Union with Christ.* Louisville: Westminster John Knox, 2007.

Husbands, Mark, and Daniel J. Treier, eds. *Justification. What's at Stake in the Current Debate?* Downer's Grove, IL: IVP, 2004.

Johnson, Marcus Peter. *One in Christ. An Evangelical Theology of Salvation.* Wheaton, IL: Crossway, 2013.

Jones, David Ceri. "Calvinistic Methodism and English Evangelicalism." In *The Emergence of Evangelicalism: Exploring Historical Continuities,* edited by Michael A. G. Haykin and Kenneth J. Stewart, pp 112-128. Nottingham: Apollos, 2008.

Kidd, Thomas S. *George Whitefield: America's Spiritual Founding Father.* New Haven: Yale University Press, 2014.

McGrath, Alister. *Iustitia Dei. A History of the Christian Doctrine of Justification.* 3rd ed. Cambridge: Cambridge University Press, 2005.

Morgan, Christopher W., and Robert A. Peterson, eds. *Hell under Fire: Modern Scholarship Reinvents Eternal Punishment.* Grand Rapids, MI: Zondervan, 2004.

Needham, Nick. "Justification in the Early Church Fathers." In *Justification in Perspective: Historical Developments and Contemporary Challenges,* edited by B. L. McCormack, 25-53. Grand Rapids, MI: Baker Academic, 2006.

Noll, Mark A. *The Rise of Evangelicalism: The Age of Edwards, Whitefield, and the Wesleys.* Downers Grove, Ill.: InterVarsity Press, 2004.

Null, Ashley. *Thomas Cranmer's Doctrine of Repentance.* Cambridge: Cambridge University Press, 2000.

Old, Hughes Oliphant. *The Reading and Preaching of the Scriptures in the Worship of the Christian Church.* Volume 5. *Modernism, Pietism, and Awakening.* Grand Rapids, MI: Eerdmans, 2005.

Packer, J. I., and Thomas Oden, eds. *One Faith: The Evangelical Consensus.* Wheaton, IL: Crossway, 2004.

Shaw, Ian J. "Nineteenth Century Perceptions." In *The Emergence of Evangelicalism: Exploring Historical Continuities,* edited by Michael A.G. Haykin and Kenneth J. Stewart. Nottingham: Apollos, 2008.

_____. *Churches, Revolutions & Empires. 1789-1914.* Fearn: Christian Focus, 2012.

Slenczka, Notger. "Luther's Anthropology." In *The Oxford Handbook of Martin Luther's Theology,* edited by Robert Kolb, Irene Dingel and L'Ubomir Batka, pp 212-232. Oxford: Oxford University Press, 2014.

Tappert, Theodore G. *The Book of Concord: The Confessions of the Evangelical Lutheran Church.* Philadelphia: Fortress Press, 2000; Orig. 1959.

Tinker, Melvin. *Salt, Light, and Cities on Hills: Evangelism and Social Action. How Do The Relate to Each Other?* (Darlington: Evangelical Press, 2014).

Trueman, Carl. "*Simul Peccator Et Justus*: Martin Luther and Justification." In *Justification in Perspective*, edited by Bruce L. McCormack, pp 73-98. Grand Rapids, MI: Baker, 2006.

Walls, Jerry L. "Heaven and Hell." In *The Oxford Handbook of Philosophical Theology*, edited by Thomas P. Flint and Michael C. Rea, pp 491-511. Oxford: OUP, 2009.

Webster, John. "*Rector Et Iudex Super Omnia Genera Doctrinarum?* The Place of the Doctrine of Justification." In *What Is Justification About? Reformed Contributions to an Ecumenical Theme*, edited by Michael Weinrich and John P. Burgess, pp 35-56. Grand Rapids, MI: Eerdmans, 2009.

Whitefield, George. *Select Sermons of George Whitefield M.A.: With an Account of His Life by J.C. Ryle and a Summary of His Doctrine by R. Elliot*. London: Banner of Truth Trust, 1959.

5. George Whitefield and Africa: Personal Reflections
by David Seccombe

In the year of our Lord 1993 I found myself unexpectedly called by the Church of England in Southern Africa (called of God, I believe) to become the Principal of a certain George Whitefield College, being myself not intimately acquainted with the history of the said George Whitefield, nor indeed overly much with the Church of England in Southern Africa. And yet what I did know of that great man caused me to think that it was a good name under which I served, and there were moments in the midst of a busy life when I managed to take up this or that volume and read a little of his life.

Such was his life that I cannot recall ever reading a page that I was not arrested by some detail or anecdote that excited or challenged me, except, I confess, once when I undertook to read one of his sermons, when I fell asleep in the midst of it, and thought afterwards that there must have been some little difference between the bare words and the manner of their being spoken.

At the end of my first year at the College named for this George Whitefield I had occasion to make my first journey to America, a journey, which, as I remember, took some half a day (it took Whitefield himself about two months), and I found myself invited to preach at a certain Episcopal Church in Charleston, South Carolina, named for St Philip the Evangelist. There was no little excitement when it was announced that I came from 'George Whitefield College' in South Africa, for, as several congregants explained to me afterwards, had not the same George Whitefield preached in this very church? Moreover, as I was shaking hands with people at the door a man took out his wallet and wrote me a $1000 cheque for 'my poor orphans' in Cape Town. So I thought not too much had changed.

I was interested then, when I returned to Cape Town to learn more of George Whitefield's ministry in Charleston, so repaired to the journals of that man, and read to my surprise, that although I believe it is indeed so that he attended St Philip's Church on three successive Sundays, it was to hear himself denounced from the pulpit, and on another occasion was summoned to appear there before the Bishop of London's commissary to answer certain charges to do with the welfare of his soul. So his ministry in Charleston was thenceforth among Congregationalists and others, and our Baptist brothers will be interested to know that whereas the Baptist community in that city was fallen to a handful of souls, from the time of Mr. Whitefield's ministry among them it has never ceased to flourish.

So in the year of our Lord 2010, when providence appointed that I should address the new students at the occasion of their boot camp, it seemed good to deliberate why the college founders should have chosen the name George Whitefield. I confess the more to drawing on my own instincts than on careful research, and, perhaps happily, I am not able to find my notes from that time. Nevertheless, as I recall it, I saw the reasons as follows.

First and foremost was that George Whitefield was a preacher of the gospel of salvation in Christ. The Church of England in South Africa has a tradition of evangelical preaching. Reference has been made to the revival that God brought about in Cape Town in the 1970's through the preaching of the young Frank Retief. His friend, Joe Bell, was preaching with passion in KwaZulu Natal, and there were others who followed in the tradition of Rev R.G. Lamb, whom Bishop Robert Gray moved from what became St. George's Cathedral, to quote Gray's words, to weaken 'the low element in Cape Town' (the evangelicals). Lamb continued to minister fruitfully at Holy Trinity Gardens, to the degree that, according to the late Bishop Stephen Bradley, a quarter of the Christian population of Cape Town attributed their salvation to the preaching of Paddy Lamb. GWC's founders wished above all that graduates of this College should preach the gospel of the grace of God in Jesus Christ.

Several other things commended his name. He was a Bible preacher. He preached the great doctrines of the faith, most especially the reformation doctrines of justification by faith, and the basis of our salvation in the finished work of Christ. He was, of course, a minister of the Church of England, but was possessed of an ecumenical spirit, such that he was happy to fellowship with and work alongside anyone and everyone who loved Christ and professed his gospel. And then, I told the students, he had a social conscience, founding an orphanage in the colony of Georgia and collecting money whenever he preached for 'my orphans', as he called them.

I was thinking to myself the talk had gone well, when a certain Zulu first year student, Gerald Mbebe by name, approached and asked me 'did I know that George Whitefield owned slaves?'. I had to confess to some acquaintance with the fact, but I had clearly airbrushed it from the portrait I remembered and had just drawn. Embarrassing! But I remembered another of my Christian heroes, Thomas Cranmer, the Archbishop of Canterbury, who was burned at the stake because he refused to concede that the bread and wine of the Lord's Supper were really transformed into the Lord's body and blood at the words of the priest. Led to the stake in Oxford Cranmer was heard to be confessing his sins. I recall my confusion at this when as a very new Christian I read his story in Bishop Ryle's little masterpiece, *Five English Reformers*. Why would a man, who was about to be burned alive for his faith in Christ, be confessing his sins? At the time I did not have a strong conviction of my own sinfulness. But Cranmer had many sins and compromises, and I recall my discomfort when I read of them. Similarly Martin Luther and John Calvin. All our heroes crumble under close scrutiny.

I ministered for a time under an Indian priest from the Anglo-Catholic tradition, but with a strong evangelical preaching ministry. In a public forum he was once asked what he thought about the saints. He answered that all men are sinners, and that if we viewed them closely we would see that it was so. The saints, he said, were people who excelled in some particular facet of their lives. They were still sinners, needing to be saved by the grace of God. Whitefield had serious blind spots; my wife gets angry about his neglect of his wife. The real lesson to be learned is about ourselves: do we see our own compromises, and the corruption of our own hearts and minds? How will people view us in one hundred years time? How perhaps do some view us now? If we disqualify sinners, we disqualify everyone. Original sin is not just original; it is a corruption of our nature that reaches to our depths, and will only be eradicated in full by a supernatural transformation when we enter into glory.

I am not a Whitefield scholar. I went to the library to find a biography to read something for this occasion. All the books were out, except an old one by Joseph Belcher, dated 1857.[1] I did not have time to read it in full, but as I said before, when reading of Whitefield every page holds a lesson, a challenge, and something to ponder. There are numerous references to his ministry to 'negroes', as the author calls them. 'Many negroes came to the evangelist with the inquiry, "have I a soul?" and a church was formed ... No less than one hundred and forty were received as constituent members of the church, and large additions were made from time to time to their number'.[2] It is worthy of

---

[1] Joseph Belcher, *George Whitefield: A Biography. With Special Reference to His Labours in America* (New York, NY: American Tract Society, 1857).
[2] Belcher, *Whitefield*, p 130.

note that at a time when many wished to place coloured people outside of the human race (hence fair game for every form of exploitation), George Whitefield and many other Christians – including the Pope – insisted on their humanity because they were capable of a relationship with God.

There was a drinking club in the city of Philadelphia, which had attached to itself a negro boy entertainer with a remarkable gift of mimicry. One day the gentlemen asked him to imitate George Whitefield. The boy did not want to, but they pushed him and he did his best. But the spirit of the man must surely have come upon him – or the Spirit of God – for he rose up and preached to them as the Whitefield himself: 'I speak the truth in Christ, I lie not; unless you repent, you will all be damned'. Laughter gradually turned to silence. The club broke up and never met again.[3]

What of George Whitefield and Africa? How thankful I am for those who have organized this Symposium and to those who have spoken! What profit there is to be had from study of the lives of great men! As long as I have been associated with this College there has been in the back of my mind – sometimes in the front – the thought that God could raise up a George Whitefield for Africa: 'God's cavalryman'. I was taken by this thought from Lee Gatiss. I agree that it is the sentinels who lead the local churches who are the real key to the coming of the kingdom of God. But how easily the churches get to looking after their own affairs, and cease to affect the unbelieving masses. It was so then, and it is so now. Hundreds of thousands of people who would never have come inside a church to hear of the Saviour were drawn by curiosity to listen to Whitefield in the fields – and found eternal life. When I studied theology in the late 1960's at Moore College in Sydney, one quarter of the students had embraced Christ in the Billy Graham Crusades of 1959 and 1964. My own mother was an indirect convert. So many attended out of curiosity – critical, often to make fun. But God intended differently.

Could we produce another George Whitefield? Let me ask it another way: Was there ever another like George Whitefield? I think of Benjamin Franklin, the sceptic, working his way back through the crowds in the market square in Philadelphia, listening, calculating, and deciding that Whitefield could be heard clearly by 30,000 people in the open air. And the old man recalling hearing Whitefield's clearly

[3] Belcher, *Whitefield*, p 131.

pronounced speech at a distance of two miles. So, no, but yes, there was once such a one. Luke tells us in the 8th chapter of his Gospel that so many tens of thousands pressed upon Jesus to hear him that some were even trampled. That man could hold the attention of a vast crowd all day. But then, just to make the comparison is to understand that the raising up of such a one does not lie within our grasp, but must wait upon the sovereign providence of God.

5.1. What can we learn then from this remarkable man?

Firstly we can be reminded and encouraged about the power of the preached gospel, when God moves in mercy to open people's hearts by his Holy Spirit. But should we not consider that these things go together? When God in his sovereign purpose determines he will have mercy on a people, he will both raise up the preachers and move in power to confirm their words in the hearts of hearers. So when we see God bringing forward men and women who are eager to proclaim his gospel – to which this College is a testimony – he will also work with them to bring about his purpose of mercy. It is in his hands whether it will be another Whitefield or an army of poor preachers such as went throughout England at the time of John Wycliffe.

The second thing to learn is that understanding the full range of biblical doctrine is not above and beyond the ordinary man, woman and child. Whitefield has shown us that Christian doctrine is to be preached to all and is powerful to reach the hearts of the simplest. The doctrines of God and of the Trinity and of the person and work of Christ and the Holy Spirit and predestination and justification and sanctification and the Christian life and the kingdom of God and the church and ministry and sacraments are for preaching and for transforming ordinary people's lives.

Third, consider Whitefield's pastoral concern. He may not have set up classes like John Wesley, but everywhere he preached the Christian life, counselled, and encouraged faithful ministers to their task. I could add here that he was enthusiastic and appreciative of the ministry of the theological school. He says of the Log College, the first theological college to be established in America and the forerunner of Princeton:

> The place wherein the young men study now, is in contempt called "the college". It is a long-house about twenty feet long, and nearly as many broad; and to me it seemed to resemble the school of the old prophets, for their habitations were mean. That they sought not great things for themselves is plain from these passages of

Scripture, wherein we are told that each of them took a beam to build them a house; and that at the feast of the sons of the prophets, one of them put on the pot, while the others went to fetch some herbs out of the field. All that we can say of most of our universities is, they are glorious without. From this despised place, seven or eight worthy ministers of Jesus have lately been sent forth; more are almost ready to be sent, and the foundation is now laying for the instruction of many others.[4]

Fourth, notwithstanding what we have said about the very real sinfulness of us all, George Whitefield included, let us be encouraged by the life of a man who was totally sold out to the business of his Lord. It seems he was never too tired, or troubled by his asthma, that if there were people needing help he would not seek to help them. The account of his life gives the impression of a man as selfless as it is possible to imagine a sinful man to be. We will always harbour suspicion of someone who spends a lot of time in the limelight, and whose preaching manner is theatrical, that he basks in the glory and is essentially self-motivated. But it is the length and consistency of Whitefield's ministry, which dispels that notion. The extraordinary story of his last night shows that to his dying day he ministered not to glorify himself but to persuade souls to Jesus. Worn out and on his way to bed, witnesses said that he stopped on the stairs, and with a lighted candle in one hand, preached for more than an hour to the people gathered at the house. He died later that night.

Fifth, let us take heed of his ecumenical spirit. At Moore College in Sydney and here at GWC I experienced in two unashamedly Anglican foundations an openness, a respect, and an affection for the work that God was doing in other denominational families, and a desire to make available what God has given to us to whomever should be helped by it. I thought we owed this spirit to my predecessor Broughton Knox, but discovered here in South Africa that the same attitude imbued the Church of England, which saw its mission not as building an Anglican denomination, but as helping to grow the kingdom of God. I realize from this symposium that they inherited this spirit, and we owe it today to George Whitefield, who was born in the year of our Lord, 1714, and died at the age of 55 in the year familiar to every Australian schoolboy when Captain James Cook planted the British flag at Botany Bay.

---

[4] Belcher, *Whitefield*, p 105.

Sixth, an eye towards the material needs of the wider communities God places us in, is yet another lead we can take from Whitefield. Albeit his blind spots (and don't we all have them), the notion of Christianity 'with a soft edge' is part of his legacy. I learned that expression from a man here in Muizenberg, who pleaded with me that we did not ignore the many needy people around us as we went about our theological training mission. Here in Africa a concern for the poor should accompany our zeal for the gospel.

Seventh, and I am thinking here as a College principal, though our traditional wisdom tells us that theological studies are best not undertaken until a person develops a level of maturity, say between 24 and 30, we should be alert to the fact that God will sometimes lay his hand on someone much younger. Whitefield, Spurgeon and others should teach us flexibility in judging people's gifts and potential. I suspect that a great part of the power of Whitefield's fearless directness with people came through his beginning to preach so young.

Last, let us never forget that it is Jesus and his kingdom that we serve, and that he is the King and Commander-in-Chief. He entrusts to us much, but remains in sovereign control of how his kingdom grows. Revival is within his power to grant. We should never become so discouraged by the deterioration of spiritual things around us that we give up believing. God has wrought a miracle in Africa in the past century, not by raising up a Whitefield, but by touching a multitude of ordinary Africans and sending them to their fellows with similar zeal and spirit of self-sacrifice for the gospel. There are students sitting in this room who can tell you stories of how God has blessed their labours in preaching and is continuing to raise up a great harvest of the saved.

5.2. Sources

Belcher, Joseph. *George Whitefield: A Biography. With Special Reference to His Labours in America.* New York, NY: American Tract Society, 1857.

6. George Whitefield and Revival: Scotland 1741-42
by Ian J. Shaw

In 1835, the English Congregationalist minister Andrew Reed had a rather unusual encounter with George Whitefield (1714–1770). It was unusual not least because it took place over sixty years after Whitefield's death, and in North America, where Reed was visiting as a delegate of the English Congregational churches. He had been an admirer of George Whitefield since his youth; in England he had preached from pulpits in which Whitefield had preached; and he had read books from his library. But little was to prepare him for just how close to Whitefield he was to come on this visit. Reed's American tour took him to the church in Newbury Port, Massachusetts, where George Whitefield was buried. His party was led down into the vault where stood three coffins, that of Whitefield in the middle. His host, as was the custom of the time, then slid back the lid and there before Reed's eyes was the skeleton of his great hero, George Whitefield himself. He had hardly recovered from his surprise at this sight when his host leant into the coffin, lifted out Whitefield's skull, and handed it to Andrew Reed as the honoured guest! With characteristic understatement Reed recorded his shock – 'I could say nothing; but thought and feeling were busy!'.[1]

This chapter is a rather different sort of encounter with Whitefield, with a focus on him during a period of revival in Scotland in the early 1740s. Nonetheless, it is hoped that as a result of exploring these events, 'thought and feeling' will be busy. Whitefield was probably the greatest preacher in the 'Evangelical Revival' as it is known in Britain, or the 'Great Awakening' as it is known in America. The approach he took in preaching, and its impact on religious experience, was to play a decisive role in shaping the development of evangelicalism, building on its Reformation and Puritan roots. It also played a significant part in the way revival developed in Scotland.

A number of key features of evangelicalism were reflected in Whitefield's preaching. The first was an emphasis on the Bible. His sermons are full of biblical quotations, references, and allusions. His congregations followed the scripture passage as it was read, and looked

---

[1] I.J. Shaw, *The Greatest is Charity: Andrew Reed (1787-1862), Preacher and Philanthropist*, (Darlington: Evangelical Press, 2005), p 152.

up the verses he quoted. On his first visit to Scotland in 1741 he preached to Ralph Erskine's congregation in Dunfermline, and he recalled – 'after I had done prayer and named my text, the rustling made by opening the Bibles all at once quite surprised me; a scene I never was witness to before'.[2]

The Evangelical Revival also brought supernatural religion to a society dominated by Deism, the belief that God was there, but played little role in the world or the lives of ordinary people. Evangelicals in the eighteenth century stressed the direct intervention of God. This was part of the dramatic appeal of Whitefield's preaching to his audiences – he brought God's word to bear on their lives. Whitefield dealt with individuals directly, speaking of repentance, conversion, new birth. The experience of God he spoke about was immediate and personal. Another evangelical emphasis seen in Whitefield was upon justification by God's grace alone, through faith. Indeed, his first sermon in Glasgow in 1741, entitled 'The Lord our Righteousness,' was a classic presentation of justification by faith alone.[3]

Preaching was central to the Evangelical Revival, with a stress on the need for personal conversion. This meant preaching for a decision, which brings a life change. Whitefield was above all else a preacher: he centred on biblical certainties, heaven and hell, Christ and the Cross; the difference between true and nominal faith. Although he was decidedly an Anglican, and regularly made clear his conformity to Anglican forms,[4] he also notably operated on the principles of evangelical ecumenism – during the Evangelical Revival he also worked with Presbyterians, Independents, and Moravians.

As an evangelical Calvinist he felt at home in Presbyterian Scotland. Although an Episcopalian, he accommodated his practice to the local context so as to become acceptable. In a letter written when he was in Scotland in July 1742 he declared he was not prepared to go as far as some wished and renounce the Church of England, but he observed, 'I have shown my freedom in communicating with the Church of

---

[2] G. Whitefield, 'Letter 337, to Mr. J____ C____, 1 August, 1741', in *Works of George Whitefield*, Vol. 1, (London: E&C Dilly, 1771), pp 304-305.
[3] G. Whitefield, 'The Lord Our Righteousness,' A Sermon Preached on Friday Forenoon, September 11th 1741, in the High Church Yard of Glasgow', in *Works of Whitefield*, Vol. 5.
[4] See chapter 1 in this volume by Lee Gatiss.

Scotland, and in baptising children their own way'.[5] During the Presbyterian communion season[6] at Cambuslang in 1742 he was invited by the local Presbyterian ministers to help distribute the bread and wine. Despite reminding them he was an ordained Anglican minister, the invitation was renewed, and he accepted and actively participated.[7] Theologically, Whitefield was an evangelical Calvinist, but he was willing to work with Arminians, including John and Charles Wesley. Such ecclesiological and theological co-operation set the tone for what evangelicalism has become – a movement running across and through the heart of denominations, rather than separating into a single denomination. Whitefield helped to shape evangelicalism as a movement of like-minded believers who agree on the major things, and disagree on secondary matters, and on this basis are willing to work together.[8]

A notable incident occurred near the start of Whitefield's first visit to Scotland in 1741, which in many ways proved a defining moment. He had been invited to preach north of the border by two men, Ebenezer Erskine (1680-1754) and his brother Ralph (1685-1752). They led a group of thoroughgoing evangelicals who had seceded from the Church of Scotland to form the Associate Presbytery. They felt that evangelicalism was being hindered by staying within the established Church of Scotland, although the flash point became the demand that congregations be allowed to choose their own minister (rather than it being the choice of the church patron – who was often the landowner). After he arrived, it became clear to Whitefield that their invitation was to preach only in their Associate Presbytery churches, and nowhere else. They did not want him to engage in the open, denominationally mixed, mass preaching he had undertaken in the American colonies. Whitefield's response shows the breadth of his heart, as he declared he came 'only as an occasional preacher, to preach the simple Gospel, to all

---

[5] G. Whitefield, 'Letter 429 to Rev. Mr. W____, of Dundee, 7 July 1742,' in *Works of Whitefield*, Vol. 1, p 406.

[6] The 'communion season' was a tradition in Scottish Presbyterianism of a series of meetings from a Friday to a Monday building up to the communion service itself on the Sunday, and then reflection and consecration on Monday. They were only held 2 to 4 times a year, and were important spiritual and social events. The communion service was held within the communion season, but the two things are not the same, hence the different terminology.

[7] *Works of Whitefield*, Vol. 1, p 407.

[8] See Roger H. Martin, *Evangelicals United: Ecumenical Stirrings in Pre-Victorian Britain, 1795-1830*, Studies in Evangelicalism 4, (London: Scarecrow Press, 1983) for an outline of the shaping influence of Whitefield's legacy on 'pan-evangelicalism' in the decades succeeding his death.

that are willing to hear me, of whatever denomination'. He added, 'if the Pope himself would lend me his pulpit, I would gladly proclaim the righteousness of Christ therein'.[9]

This stance closed the door to the Associate Presbytery – although many of their members did come to hear him, and some converts eventually joined their churches. He preached instead for a group of Church of Scotland ministers who had already begun to see God moving in revival in their church. Whitefield's choice in this matter helped to shape evangelicalism in Scotland, preventing it from becoming tied to one particular denomination, and helping to ensure that there was an evangelical stream in the Church of Scotland thereafter.

All this meant that George Whitefield's preaching, together with his theological and ecclesiological approach, proved very significant in shaping evangelicalism. The fact that these issues were worked out in the context of revival, in which narrowly held denominational or theological views appear less important, is notable.

6.1. The nature of revival

In its understanding of the nature of revival, this chapter follows the view found in the writings of Jonathan Edwards, that it is 'a surprising' work of God. He would probably have used the word 'awakening', rather than revival, and by that referred to aspects of the spiritual renewal of Christians, conversions in large numbers, and the furtherance of mission.

Josh Moody expresses this well in his recent study of Jonathan Edwards, *The God-Centred Life*, based on his Cambridge PhD:

> Revival encapsulates the supreme work of God invading space-time with his powerful presence. Revivals are echoes of that great revival wrought through Jesus Christ, and applied through the gift of the Holy Spirit at Pentecost... Revival is not organized by humans. But nor is revival simply an arbitrary or unusual mechanism of God for unexpected moments... revival means nothing more or less than *salvation* applied and extraordinarily promoted.[10]

---

[9] George Whitefield, 'Letter 280, to Mr E___ E___ at Sterling' (sic), from Bristol, May 16, 1741, in *Works of Whitefield*, Vol. 1, p 262; 'Letter, 339, to Mr Thomas N___, New York', from Edinburgh, August 8, 1741, in *Works of Whitefield*, Vol. 1, p 308.

[10] J. Moody, *The God-Centred Life: Insights from Jonathan Edwards for Today* (Leicester: IVP, 2006), p 34.

Jonathan Edwards, with his incredible mind, wrote much about the events of revival, and subjected them to close analysis. He spoke of 'awakening' as God's sovereign work, but also promoted the 'Concert for Prayer' to encourage united efforts for prayer for revival.[11] This means that 'awakening' is 'surprising' when it comes, but may not be totally spontaneous. People pray for it, preach sermons to prepare for it, circulate literature and accounts about it, invite well-known preachers to preach – as they did when Whitefield was invited to Scotland – but when it comes it is still surprising, and to a degree unexpected. Whitefield uses the term 'revival' at least 8 times in his *Journals*, usually speaking of 'a revival of religion', or 'the late revival' when speaking of these dramatic events.[12] This is different from the view of 'revival' extensively promoted in the nineteenth century by preachers and writers such as Charles Finney, who argued that revival can be organised, planned for, and made to happen by following certain approaches, plans and techniques. It is a type of thinking still found in some circles in evangelicalism, but is better termed 'revivalism'.[13] Revival itself is instead hard to define, it can be untidy, hard to control despite the best efforts of ministers, and leading to significant opposition.

In his recent book *Global Awakening: How Twentieth Century Revivals Triggered a Christian Revolution*, Mark Shaw of Africa International University, Nairobi, has argued that in assessing the phenomenal 'comeback' of Christianity globally, especially in the second half of the twentieth century, the role of revival needs to be given full credit. Revival became the 'delivery mechanism' by which missionary activity, Bible translation, contextualisation have advanced – all part of the 'the great symphony of religious revolution.' Mark Shaw contends, 'Global revivals... are at the heart of the global resurgence of Christianity'. [14] This suggests that the topic of preaching in revival remains important, and very relevant to today.

---

[11] See J. Edwards, 'An Humble Attempt to Promote Explicit Agreement and Visible Union of God's People in Extraordinary Prayer', 1747, in *Works of Jonathan Edwards*, 1834 (republ. Edinburgh: Banner of Truth, 1974, Vol II), pp 280-312.
[12] G. Whitefield, *Journals of George Whitefield 1737-1745*, 1st edn., reproduced (Oswestry: Quinta Press, 2009).
[13] See C. Finney, *Revivals of Religion: Lectures by Charles Grandison Finney*, W.H. Harding (ed.) (London: n.p., 1868).
[14] Mark Shaw, *Global Awakening: How Twentieth Century Revivals Triggered a Christian Revolution* (Downers Grove: IVP, 2010), pp 11-12.

6.2. The Evangelical revival background

In his book *Evangelicalism and Modern Britain*, David Bebbington has drawn close connections between the Evangelical Revival and the Enlightenment.[15] This strong indebtedness has been importantly challenged by a group of evangelical scholars in *The Emergence of Evangelicalism*,[16] where the continuity of evangelicalism with Puritan, Reformation, and indeed Biblical patterns, was re-asserted. Yet, the impact of the Enlightenment should not be ignored, and Douglas Sweeney offered a helpful summary when speaking of evangelicalism as being 'classical Christian orthodoxy, shaped by a largely Protestant understanding of the gospel, and distinguished from other such movements by an eighteenth century twist'.[17]

The immediate start of the Evangelical Revival is traced by W.R. Ward to Europe, with Pietists of the European continent praying for renewal amongst a Lutheranism gone cold. This saw awakenings experienced in Silesia, and then amongst groups of Lutherans near Salzburg before they were scattered by persecution, and in the Tyrol and the Baltic. Revival was then seen amongst the Moravians, who had settled on the estate of Count Nicholas von Zinzendorf in Germany in 1727. There were repeated cycles of revivals in North America and in the North East of Scotland, in the same period. Solomon Stoddart, the grandfather of Jonathan Edwards was of Puritan stock, and in his ministry at Northampton, Massachusetts he saw five periods of 'great reaping of fruit' between 1679 and 1718. The Evangelical Revival was not so much one event, but a series of community revivals which coalesced together into a pan-international movement.[18] A catalyst in that process was the preaching of George Whitefield.

6.3. George Whitefield's ministry before 1741-42

Whitefield's conversion came after a long period of intense spiritual struggle when some feared he was losing his sanity, and even his health. His testimony has echoes of the experience of Martin Luther,

---

[15] D. Bebbington, *Evangelicalism in Modern Britain: A History from the 1730s to the 1980s* (London: Unwin Hyman, 1989), pp 50-72.
[16] K. Stewart and M. Haykin (eds.), *The Emergence of Evangelicalism* (Leicester: IVP, 2008).
[17] D. Sweeney, *The American Evangelical Story* (Grand Rapids: Baker, 2005), pp 23-24.
[18] W.R. Ward, *The Protestant Evangelical Awakening* (Cambridge: Cambridge University Press, 1992), pp 54-286.

and perhaps it is deliberately described that way.[19] This pattern of spiritual crisis, anxiety, and release became the hallmark of the experience he preached for in others.[20] From the moment he first set foot in a pulpit to preach, his ministry was attended by the characteristics of revival. Whitefield's first sermon in Gloucester, the day after his ordination, had a remarkable effect. He recalled, 'as I proceeded, I perceived the fire kindled... Some few mocked, but most of those present seemed struck'. Someone complained to the bishop afterwards that the sermon 'drove fifteen mad,' which suggests they were deeply convicted or even converted.[21] Similar effects were reported as a result of his preaching in various pulpits in London, and then Bristol, in the summer of 1736 while he waited before travelling as a preaching missionary to America.

The themes Whitefield addressed in his pulpit ministry may be familiar ones to contemporary evangelicals, but not to congregations in the Eighteenth Century. His first published sermon was 'The Nature and Necessity of our Regeneration or New Birth in Christ Jesus' (1737) – which dealt with a classic theme of revival.[22] Another feature of Whitefield's preaching was its emotional intensity. He often wept in the pulpit, such that he was sometimes overwhelmed and had to stop. This was unusual to congregations often used to sermons being dry, lengthy, discourses on morality. Yet his preaching was not just emotionalism. It had a powerful impact on his audience – who also often wept.[23]

After 1737, Whitefield adopted the habit of preaching extemporary sermons, without resort to a sermon script. They were usually sermons he had preached a number of times before, but this approach became a significant, and necessary feature, at the height of revival when he was often called on to preach four times a day. The practice of field preaching had been undertaken by others before Whitefield, such as by Howell Harris, the 'Welsh exhorter,' and as London pulpits closed against him in his early ministry, Whitefield took to preaching in graveyards, public open spaces, and the fields. When he preached to the

---

[19] J. Gillies, *Memoirs of the late Reverend George Whitefield* (London: T. Williams, 1812), pp 13-14.
[20] H. Stout, *The Divine Dramatist: George Whitefield and the Rise of Modern Evangelicalism* (Grand Rapids: Eerdmans, 1991), p 28.
[21] Gillies, *Memoirs,* p 16, citing Whitefield's *Letters,* Letter XVI.
[22] The sermon is reproduced in Lee Gatiss (ed.), *Sermons of George Whitefield.* Volume 2 (Wheaton, IL: Crossway, 2012), pp 275-287.
[23] Stout, *Divine Dramatist,* p 42.

miners of Kingswood outside Bristol, a huge crowd of up to 10,000 attended.[24] Just before going to Scotland in 1741 and 1742 he had preached in the open spaces of London, at Moorfields and Kennington Common, amidst the noise and chaos of fairs, with people shouting, and blowing horns, and creating chaos and mischief. Perhaps 20,000 people gathered on occasion, yet somehow Whitefield, with his tremendous vocal capacity, was able to be heard, and see fruits from his preaching.[25]

Whitefield preached with similar success in the colonies of North America. In November 1739 he spoke out of doors in Philadelphia to a crowd of 6,000 people, roughly half the population of the city,[26] and then preached in Northampton, Massachusetts, when Jonathan Edwards was present. Whitefield reported 'Dear Mr Edwards wept during the whole time of exercise,'[27] indeed Northampton was much altered as a result of this ministry, and within a month revival had broken out again. Sarah Edwards wrote of Whitefield's preaching – 'It is wonderful to see what a spell he cast over an audience by proclaiming the simplest truths of the Bible. I have seen upwards of a thousand people hang on his words with breathless silence, broken only by a half-suppressed sob.'[28]

The account of Nathan Cole, a farmer who heard news that Whitefield was going to preach in his area, captures the sense of excitement, anticipation, and fervour of the growing revival. As Cole rushed with his wife on horseback to the scene of the preaching, he recalled, 'I saw before me a cloud or fog... as I came nearer ye road I heard a noise something like a low rumbling thunder and I presently found out it was ye rumbling of horses feet coming down ye road, and this cloud was a cloud of dust made by the running of horses' feet ... when we got down to ye old meeting house there was a great multitude it was said to be 3 or 4,000... Every horse seemed to go with all his might for the saving of souls.'[29]

---

[24] G. Whitefield, *Journals*, p 263.
[25] A. Dallimore, *George Whitefield: The Life and Times of the Great Evangelist of the Eighteenth-Century Revival* (Edinburgh: Banner of Truth, 1970), Vol. 1, pp 283-297.
[26] Whitefield, *Journals*, p 523.
[27] Whitefield, *Journals*, p 605.
[28] Quoted in L. Tyerman, *The Life of the Rev. George Whitefield* (London, Hodder and Stoughton, 1876), Vol. 1, pp 428-429.
[29] N. Cole, 'The Spiritual Travails of Nathan Cole' draft. Mss., quoted in Dallimore, *George Whitefield*, Vol. 1, p 541.

The Awakening became a movement that transcended the boundaries of the colonies, and made Whitefield an international religious personality. In places the crowds exceeded the total population of the town or village. Building on the traditions of piety and revival present in the colonies, his preaching was like introducing a naked flame to dry kindling wood.

6.4. Revival in eighteenth-century Scotland

One of most famous episodes in the Evangelical Revival of the Eighteenth Century took place in the parishes of Cambuslang and Kilsyth, each a few miles from Glasgow in Scotland. The two principal ministers involved in these events were William MacCulloch (1691-1771), and James Robe (1688-1753), who each left important accounts of events, including written testimonies from a large number of converts.

Kilsyth and Cambuslang in 1742 were parishes of a similar size, comprising large villages in which there was some early industrial development and mining, surrounded by agricultural fields, where most derived their employment. The population of Cambuslang was less than 1,000 people, and Glasgow itself was little more than a large market town, with a population of about 17,000 people. The churches in both parishes had suffered times of slow spiritual growth as well as economic problems, and had internal difficulties with disputes over leadership.[30]

In 1739 MacCulloch began preaching a series of sermons in Cambuslang on the subject of the new birth. The following year, Robe similarly began to preach on 'regeneration' in Kilsyth. This led to the demand for more teaching and preaching from the Bible. On 18 February 1742, about 50 people came to MacCulloch's house under deep conviction of sin and fearful about the state of their souls. Before long some 300 people had been converted. As the numbers increased, the congregation became of such a size that it needed to meet in the open air, on the 'preaching braes' in a bowl in the hillside near to the church. Here they regularly met for over a year. The revival in Kilsyth began in April 1742, a few weeks after the one in Cambuslang had commenced. By May 1742 it had also become a major event. Both

---

[30] A. Fawcett, *The Cambuslang Revival: The Scottish Evangelical Revival of the Eighteenth Century* (Edinburgh: Banner of Truth, 1971), provides an excellent account of the revival and its background.

revivals were therefore well under way before George Whitefield arrived in Scotland to preach that June and July.[31]

This was not his first visit. Whitefield had preached in Glasgow in the previous year, 1741, and many later converts at Cambuslang looked back on the seeds sown there as key to their conversion. His sermon in Glasgow on 'The Lord our Righteousness' stressed how Christ needed to be personally received and the message applied – 'an unapplied Christ, is no Christ at all.' As he preached the sermon his voice was so filled with emotion that he was almost sobbing – 'Alas, my heart almost bleeds! What a multitude of precious souls are now before me! How shortly must all be ushered into eternity: and yet, O cutting thought! Was God now to require all your souls, how few, comparatively speaking, could really say, *The Lord our righteousness.*' As he drew to a close, he pleaded 'Come then, poor, guilty prodigals, come home.'[32] One young woman, aged around 19, remembered in her testimony the reference to the Prodigals going into the far country – 'I thought he was just speaking to me, and was going to name me out...'[33]

Whitefield also preached in Edinburgh and the north-east of Scotland. His visit to Aberdeen in 1741 saw a remarkable occurrence which was later reported in Tyerman's biography of Whitefield. As he travelled north he heard of a widow in distress whose landlord had taken her furniture because she could not pay her rent. Whitefield heard of this and gave the widow all that he had in his purse – 5 guineas. When his friend later rebuked him for being too generous, Whitefield replied 'When God brings a case of distress before us, it is [so] that we can relieve it.' They travelled on further, and as they went a highwayman [street robber] stopped them and demanded their money. As a result of his earlier generosity, Whitefield had none to give, but the friend who had rebuked him now had to hand over his money. Whitefield ventured the comment that it was better that his money was with the poor widow than with the highwayman. They had not travelled much further when the highwayman returned and demanded

---

[31] J. Robe, *A Faithful Narrative of the Extraordinary Work of the Spirit of God at Kilsyth and Other Congregations in the Neighbourhood* (Glasgow: n.p., 1789), [See also the 1742 edn, Glasgow], p vi.

[32] G. Whitefield, 'Sermon XIV', *Works of Whitefield*, Vol. V, pp 230, 232.

[33] Mary Shaw's testimony, in W. M'Culloch, 'Examinations of persons Under Spiritual Concern at Cambuslang, during the Revival in 17-41-42, by Revd. Wm M'Culloch Minister of Cambuslang with Marginal notes by Dr Webster and other ministers'. Unpublished Manuscript, New College, University of Edinburgh, vol. II, pp 28-29.

Whitefield's coat, which he freely gave, on the condition that he received the robber's poor torn and threadbare coat in exchange, which the preacher then put on. They had not gone much further when they heard the highwayman's horse galloping up again. The friends concluded that the only thing the highwayman had left to take now was their lives, so they spurred their horses on to the nearest house for shelter. They just made it there before the highwayman did, and were ushered inside. Now safe, Whitefield took off the tattered old coat, and found wrapped in one pocket a parcel containing over £100 – the reason the man was so keen to catch up with them again![34]

George Whitefield returned to Scotland seven months after his first visit, in response to news he had heard of the growing awakening from William MacCulloch. On 15th June he preached twice in Kilsyth, reporting congregations of 10,000, and 'such a commotion surely was never heard of ... It far outdid all that I ever saw in America ... Their cries and agonies were exceedingly affecting.'[35] He then travelled on to Glasgow where he was warmly greeted. By 3 am the following morning a congregation was already gathering to hear him, and when he preached at 7am it was to 'many, many thousands'.[36] He moved on to Cambuslang where he arrived at mid-day, preached at 2pm, 6pm, 9pm then at 11 o'clock to thousands and the service continued until 2am. Whitefield reported:

> Such commotions, surely, were never heard of, especially at eleven o'clock at night. For an hour and a half there was such weepings, and so many falling into such deep distress, expressed in various ways, as cannot be described. The people seemed to be slain in scores. Their agonies and cries were exceedingly affecting. Mr M'Culloch preached after I had done, till past one in the morning, and then could not persuade the people to depart. In the fields, all night, could be heard the voice of prayer and praise... The commotions increase.[37]

Whitefield preached up to five times the following day, and then took opportunities to minister in Paisley, Irvine, Mearns, Cumbernauld and Falkirk, before travelling back to Edinburgh, delivering one, two, and

---

[34] Tyerman, *Life of Whitefield*, Vol. 1, pp 525-526.
[35] George Whitefield, 'Letter to John Cennick from Glasgow', in *Works of Whitefield*, Vol. 1, p 405.
[36] Letter to John Cennick, quoted in Tyerman, *Whitefield*, Vol. 2, p 5-6.
[37] *Weekly History*, July 3rd, 1742, quoted in Tyerman *Whitefield*, Vol. 2, p 6.

sometimes three, sermons in each location. In every place he reported large congregations, and 'the greatest commotion among the people'.[38]

The events in Scotland surprised even Whitefield. In a sermon in 1769 he looked back to an incident when he had seen ten thousand people affected 'in a moment, some with joy, others crying out "I cannot believe", others "God has given me faith", and some fainting in the arms of their friends'.[39] He later reported that what he had witnessed 'far out-did all that I ever saw in America.'[40]

In July he returned by invitation to preach at the Sabbath communion service in Cambuslang attended by some 20,000 people. Whitefield declared, 'scarce ever was such a sight seen in Scotland.' Because of the vast numbers in attendance, tents were set up, and the sacrament administered in the fields below the church. Although an Anglican minister, Whitefield was invited to assist in the distribution of the communion. On the Monday morning, he preached to some 20,000 again, and later wrote – 'I never before saw such a universal stir. The motion fled, as swift as lightening, from one end of the auditory to the other. Thousands were bathed in tears – some wringing their hands, others almost swooning, and others crying out and mourning over a pierced saviour. In the afternoon, the concern was very great.'[41]

The power of the revival produced a personal devotedness to Whitefield which troubled him. On July 27th he wrote to the respected clergyman John M'Laurin in Glasgow about 'several young ones who have acted wrong, I think, in leaving their respective employments, under parents and masters, to go after me. Be pleased to examine them and send them home.'[42]

In August 1742 Whitefield was again back in Cambuslang, and spent a further three weeks in the area. He preached at a second communion season on 15 August at Cambuslang. Some said 30,000 attended, others that it was 50,000, as ministers brought their congregations from local parishes to join the events. He reported 'though it rained very much there was a great awakening. The voice of prayer and praise was heard all night. It was supposed that between thirty and forty thousand people were

---

[38] Whitefield, 'Letter to a Friend in London, 7 July 1742,' in Tyerman, *Whitefield*, Vol. 2, p 6.
[39] G. Whitefield, *Eighteen Sermons* (London: W. Gurney, 1771), p 290.
[40] G. Whitefield, Letter 328, 7 July 1742, in *Works of George Whitefield*, Vol. 1 p 405, referring to the events of 6th July.
[41] *Weekly History*, July 3, 1743, in Tyerman, *Whitefield*, Vol. 2, p 7.
[42] Whitefield, Letter to John M'Laurin, Glasgow, 27 July 1742, in Tyerman, *Whitefield*, Vol. 2, p 22.

assembled, and that three thousand communicated ... great grace was among the people.' He also reported how the blessing that fell on his preaching also fell on other preachers, including William McCulloch: 'Not a few were awakened to a sense of sin; others had their bands loosed, and were brought into the liberty of the sons of God; and many of God's children were filled with joy and peace in believing.'[43]

Whitefield wrote from Cambuslang on 17 August 1742, 'I am blessed with far greater success than ever, and Satan roars louder. You will see, by what I here send, how the archers of different classes, shoot at me, but the Lord causes my bow to abide in strength, and enables me to triumph in every place.'[44]

On 3 October a similar communion season was held in Kilsyth which started at 8.30am and ended at 8.30pm, in which Whitefield participated, with twelve other ministers. Over the course of the day, twenty-two services were held.[45] On 6th October Whitefield wrote from Edinburgh – 'Glory be to His Great Name. We have seen much of His Power in Scotland. Last Sabbath and Monday things greater than ever were seen at Kilsyth. There is a great awakening also at 'Muthel'. I preach twice a day with great power, and walk in liberty and love.' Of the 'Muthel'[46] revival he reported the comments of William Hally (c. 1677-1754), the local minister, 'their mourning cries frequently drown my voice such that I am often obliged to stop till they compose themselves.'[47]

Whitefield left Scotland on 1st November 1742, but his presence had turned these small parish based revivals into part of a national and international phenomenon. His preaching did not create the revival in Lowland Scotland, for that was already underway before he arrived, but he connected it to what was happening in England, Wales, and North America.

6.5. The Sermons

There was a range to what Whitefield preached during the weeks he spent preaching in Scotland during the revival. He could preach strong

---

[43] Whitefield, Letter to a Friend in London, from *Glasgow Weekly History*, No. 39, in Tyerman, *Whitefield*, Vol. 2: pp 29-30.
[44] Letter to Mr Barber, August 17, 1742, in Tyerman, *Whitefield*, Vol. 2, p 24.
[45] J. Robe, *Faithful Narrative of Kilsyth*, 1742, pp 99-107.
[46] This is Muthill, Perthshire.
[47] Whitefield, Letter to a friend, Edinburgh, 6 October, in Tyerman, *Whitefield*, Vol. 2, p 32.

messages emphasising God's judgement and condemnation, reproducing the sense of terror he had experienced as an undergraduate seeking to be accepted by God. These were the feelings experienced by James Tenant, an unmarried man aged around 20, as he heard Whitefield preaching on the conversion of the Philippian jailer:

> As he spoke of the jailer's trembling and falling down and crying out 'What shall I do to be saved?', my conscience began to tell me that I was of all others lost and undone, unless he should in pity deliver me. I fell into great terror and trembled so much that I had to be supported by those near... I went to my quarters, lay in bed for an hour or so, and again went forth to the fields that I might give vent to my feelings in pleading with God... from the bottom of my heart, I saw myself to be one of the chief of sinners... in hearing Whitefield again I was seized with great fear and trembling because of the wickedness of my heart and life.[48]

Such experiences were also shared by women, as Bessie Lyon, aged 23, reported – 'I fell under such a sense of the divine wrath as to tremble and cry in agony, and I returned home in a state of very deep distress'.[49] Following a sermon one evening in the fields at Cambuslang, a young man reported how he

> fell into a swoon, (tho' I did not cry any) a horror of great darkness coming over me... And in the middle of this Swoon, my bodily eyes being shut, I thought I saw a clear light all at once shining about me as when the sun shines bright at Noon, and apprehended that I was in a very large room. There was represented to my mind a very large scroll of papers, let down as from the room above, fulling the breadth of the room... and it appeared to be printed all over in large distinct lines and letters. But when I thought I essayed to read I found I could not read... Only it was impressed on my mind that was a scroll containing all my Sins that were all marked and recorded before God. And after a little the Scroll was drawn up again, and I recovered out of my swoon.[50]

Yet, this was not the only tone Whitefield adopted. When he preached on 'Thy Maker is Thy Husband,' considered the most powerful sermon

---

[48] Testimony of James Tenant at Cambuslang, in D. MacFarlan, *The Revivals of the Eighteenth Century Particularly at Cambuslang* (John Johnstone, Edinburgh, n.d.), pp 167-169.
[49] Bessie Lon, quoted in MacFarlan, *Revivals of the Eighteenth Century*, pp 188-189.
[50] Quoted in Stout, *Divine Dramatist*, pp 153-154.

of the revival – he recalled how, wherever he walked after the sermon, 'you might have heard persons praying to, and praising God. The children of God came from all quarters'. The theme of the sermon was of the believer being 'married to Jesus Christ' – with an emphasis less on sin and condemnation, and more on the attractiveness of the Saviour. Whitefield found how speaking of the love and compassion of God proved powerful, as did using maternal images to comfort souls. He described his mission as being to 'take a wife for his Master's son,' and asked if there were any who 'wanted to take Christ for their husband.' Those who would come would be married 'to Christ.'[51]

A widow aged 26 heard this sermon, and found the invitation to be married to Christ overwhelming – 'I found My self just sick of love to Christ: and was made to believe that my Maker was my Husband.'[52] The concept of union with Christ was profoundly significant. Another young unmarried man, Daniel McLarty, reported:

> I felt love to Christ in my Soul, and so much joy that the sweet offers of Christ as a husband to my Soul that the joy of my heart had almost made me cry out among the people, ... after the sermon, meeting with a lady of my acquaintance, who knew I had been under Exercise, I just flew with my Arms about her, and said, such a minister has married my Soul to Christ. And I lay down on the Brae, and I was so filled with the Love of Christ and contempt of the World, that I even wished, if it were the Lord's will, that I might die on the spot.[53]

From the many thousands who attended, M'Culluch believed that there were some 500 converts at the height of the revival in 1742. In total, over two years, around 3,000 conversions were reported. However, the scope of the revival went far beyond Cambuslang, or Kilsyth, although that is where the most dramatic and climactic events took place. Many of those affected had travelled to the two centres of revival from neighbouring parishes. There were also significant revivals taking place in other locations across the Scottish Lowlands, as Whitefield observed, 'A great company of awakened souls is within the compass of twenty miles, and the work seems to be spreading apace.'[54]

---

[51] Testimony of R. Barclay, quoted in MacFarlan, *Revivals of the Eighteenth Century*, pp 157-162.
[52] W. M'Culloch, *Unpublished Manuscript*, Vol. I, p 13.
[53] Daniel McLarty's testimony in M'Culloch, *Examinations MSS*, Vol.II: 163.
[54] *Weekly History*, July 3, 1743, in Tyerman, *Whitefield*, Vol. 2, p 7.

Although MacCulloch reported that the revivals were marked by a tremendous solemnness and seriousness, the sign of 'profound reverence' for what God was doing, one aspect of the Kilsyth and Cambuslang revivals was the physical effects upon people as they responded to the preaching. They reported a sense of intense conviction of sin during the revival, and some people cried out, some fell to the ground, others trembled violently. To a number of observers in staid Presbyterian Scotland, this was quite alarming.[55]

The Lanarkshire ministers knew of Jonathan Edwards' work in New England through his *Faithful Narrative of Surprising Conversions* (1737). In this Edwards had described similar scenes to those in Scotland, with some people calling out, falling to the ground, experiencing religious ecstasies. These were seized on by opponents to discredit the whole movement.[56] As a man of the enlightenment, Edwards stressed the need for discernment, and understanding of what was, and wasn't, a work of God. In his *Treatise Concerning Religious Affections*, Edwards asserted that true religion was experiential – 'true religion in good part, consists in holy affections'. To Edwards, conversion was the impact of God on the soul, and the person's knowledge and experience of that. The signs of that taking place were genuine religious affections, which included emotional intensity of experience. These could be weeping, or bodily affections; deepened interest in religious doctrine; heightened interest in the Bible; the appearance of a loving nature. Although there might be other causes for some of these experiences, he concluded that when God is at work, 'there is no reason why a view of God's glory should not cause the body the faint.'[57]

Robe and MacCulloch corresponded with Edwards, and sent him reports of events in Scotland. They attempted to follow Edwards in capturing the essence of what was going on by recording it in written form, and analysing it. Robe kept a regular journal, extracts of which he published every couple of weeks, to inform a wider audience of the

---

[55] B. Hindmarsh, *The Evangelical Conversion Narrative: Spiritual Autobiography in Early Modern England* (Oxford, Oxford University Press, 2005), p 61.
[56] E.g. C. Chauncy, *Seasonable Thoughts on the State of Religion in New England: A Treatise in Five Parts* (Boston, Rogers and Fowle for Samuel Eliot, 1743).
[57] J. Edwards, *Select Works of Jonathan Edwards, Volume 3, The Religious Affections (1746)* (repr. London, Banner of Truth, 1961), pp 54, 60.

revival unfolding.[58] At Cambuslang, MacCulloch's approach was even more directly empirical. He chose to report the events of the revival through the words of the participants themselves, recording in detail their personal accounts and testimonies. He produced a two volume manuscript containing the fruit of these interviews in the aftermath of the revival, in which the experiences of some 110 individuals are recorded.[59] It has been called Scotland's first oral history project. Of 110 conversions that MacCulloch recorded, 75 were women, the majority of whom were unmarried. The collection of testimonies indicates that people of all ages were affected by events at Cambuslang. Some were under 10 years old, others over 70, but the largest number were aged between 13 and 24.[60]

As had happened in New England, Robe and M'Culloch also witnessed various physical and psychological manifestations during the revivals in Cambuslang and Scotland. Some reported shaking, trembling, falling to the ground, or crying out. The experiences were by no means universal. James Kirkland declared 'Yet I never fell into swarfing or fainting.'[61] To some these were evidence of hysteria, or even satanic activity. Robe and M'Culloch sought to discern what was genuine religious experience, and what was not: 'The bodies of some of the Awakened are seized with Trembling, Fainting, Histerism in some few women, with Convulsive motions in some others, arising from that Apprehension and Fear of the Wrath of God they are convinced they are under, and liable to, because of their Sins'.[62] Robe argued they were neither proof that a person was under the influence of the Spirit of God, nor did they prove they were a delusion.[63] Each experience was tested, to see whether they were of lasting value. Some cried out, some complained of terrible bodily pains (some women believed worse than

---

[58] J. Robe, *Narrative of the Extraordinary Work of the Spirit of God at Cambuslang, Kilsyth, etc. begun 1742.* Written by J. Robe and others. With attestations by ministers, preachers, etc – Glasgow, 1751 edn, (repr W. Collins, Glasgow, 1840), p xix. Sections of this are also found in J. Gillies (ed.), *Historical collections relating to remarkable periods of the success of the gospel* [1754] (revised edn 1845) (Edinburgh: Banner of Truth, 1981).

[59] MacCulloch's manuscript was donated to the New College library, Edinburgh, in the early nineteenth century, where it is still kept.

[60] J. Robe, *Narrative* (1751 edn), p 39. For a social analysis of the accounts collected by M'Culloch, see T.C. Smout, 'Born Again At Cambuslang: New Evidence On Popular Religion And Literacy In Eighteenth-Century Scotland', *Past and Present* (1982) 97 (1): pp 114-127.

[61] MacCulloch, MSS, vol. i. 364.

[62] Robe, *Narrative*, (1751 edn), p vi.

[63] Robe, *Narrative*, (1751 edn), p xii.

those in childbirth), some trembled, others fell to the ground, and a number reported seeing visions. All were fully reported and carefully assessed. Neither Robe, nor M'Culloch, nor Whitefield, believed glory would come to God if spurious religious experience were passed off as true.[64] Not all who experienced these manifestations went on to genuine conversion.[65] Robe and M'Culloch both stressed that the primary reason for the experiences many felt was the result of the preaching of the Bible.[66]

6.6. Opposition

Nonetheless, the revival and these dramatic experiences produced bitter opposition. Some of the most extreme criticism came from those who had initially invited Whitefield to Scotland. At the height of the awakening, on 15 July 1742, the Associate Presbytery declared a 'Public Fast', declaring that the 'bitter outcryings, faintings, severe bodily pains, convulsions, voices, visions and revelations' were 'a proof that the work was a delusion and of the devil.'[67] Another pamphlet followed a month later, denouncing Whitefield in the strongest terms as 'an abjured,, prelatic hireling, of as lax principles as any ever set up for the advancing of the kingdom of Satan... a base English impostor ... a poor, vainglorious, self-seeking, puffed-up creature ... a boar and a wild beast from the anti-Christian field of England, come to waste and devour the poor erring people of Scotland.'[68]

Whitefield referred to this fierce opposition from his one-time friends in a letter of October 6th, 1742 – 'the dear Messrs Erskine have dressed me in very black colours. Dear men, I pity them. Surely they must grieve the Holy Spirit much... I think, it is my one single aim to promote the kingdom of Jesus, without partiality and without hypocrisy ... I care not if the name of George Whitefield be banished out of the

---

[64] Robe, *Narrative* (1751 edn), Second Volume, p 80, pp 130-150; J. Robe, *A Short Account of the Remarkable Conversions at Cambuslang*, (Glasgow: n.p.,1742), pp 6-7.
[65] Robe, *Short Account*, p 11.
[66] Robe, *Narrative* (1751 edn), pp xv-xvi.
[67] Tyerman, *Whitefield*, Vol. 2, p 10.
[68] 'The Declaration, Protestation, and testimony of the Suffering Remnant of the anti-Popish, anti-Lutheran, anti-Prelatic, anti-Whitefieldian, anti-Erastian, anti-Sectarian, true Presbyterian Church of Christ' – quoted in Tyerman, *Whitefield*, Vol. 2, p 11.

world, that Jesus be exalted in it.'[69] Colonel Gardiner, of the British army, a strong Christian with whom Whitefield was in correspondence, put the hostility Whitefield bore into perspective in a letter to Philip Doddridge of Northampton – 'If my heart deceives me not, I would rather be the persecuted, despised Whitefield, to be an instrument in the hand of the Spirit, for converting so many souls, and building up others in their most holy faith, than be the Emperor of the whole world.'[70] Rarely is there a genuine revival without it being spoken against, sometimes most severely, and not always by those outside the Christian fold.

6.7. Assessment

The detailed information we have about Whitefield's work during the revival in Scotland allows scope for analysis of some of the issues raised about his preaching. In his book the *Divine Dramatist*, Harry Stout has argued that 'the key to understanding Whitefield is the stage,' and that he changed the sermon from a 'bookish lecture to a powerful dramatic performance.' His ability to fuse preaching and acting enabled him to spell-bind the audience.[71] In Whitefield's hands, the pulpit was transformed 'into a sacred theatre that vitally re-presented the lives of biblical saints and sinners to his captivated listeners.'[72]

Certainly, Whitefield's preaching in Scotland was different to the usual Presbyterian fare – there was more application, illustration, and emotion. He undoubtedly had greater dramatic and oratorical skills than M'Culloch or Robe, neither of whom were noted as particularly lively preachers. Yet the revival had started long before Whitefield arrived, and so their preaching abilities were already being effectively used, and the testimonies recorded attribute many conversions to their preaching as well as that of their more illustrious visitor. There is no evidence Robe or MacCulloch tried in any way to imitate Whitefield. In Scotland, the key to Whitefield's success is less 'the stage,' or 'dramatic performance' as Stout suggested, and more to do with his ability to adapt himself to the context and fit in with what God was already doing.

---

[69] Whitefield, Letter from Edinburgh, 6 October, 1742; quoted in Tyerman, *Whitefield*, Vol. 2, p 33.
[70] *Correspondence of Philip Doddridge*, Vol. IV, p 113; quoted in Tyerman, *Whitefield*, Vol. 2, p 34.
[71] Stout, *Divine Dramatist*, Foreword, p x.
[72] Stout, *Divine Dramatist*, p 44.

He and his Scottish friends would have seen what was happening not as great talents being deployed, but as the Holy Spirit bringing fruit from faithful gospel labours in a new and 'surprising' way. Genuine preaching should include life and emotion, and feeling, without it needing to become a theatrical performance.

Another criticism levelled at Whitefield's preaching concerns its emotionalism. In his magnum opus, *A History of Christianity*, Diarmaid McCulloch speaks of 'the emotional havoc caused in congregations in the wake of Whitefield's visits.'[73] Dr Alexander Webster of Edinburgh interpreted events in different ways. He wrote of the 'solemn Reverence which o'erspreads every countenance' when Whitefield preached.

> They hear as Creatures made for eternity, who don't know but next moment must account to their great Judge. Thousands are melted down into Tears; – Many cry out in Bitterness of their Soul ... Talk of a precious Christ, ALL seem to breathe after him. These, *dear Sir*, are the visible Effects of this *extraordinary Work*.[74]

Whitefield did not encourage the dramatic experiences that Robe and M'Culloch recorded, and they seemed to happen as much under the ministry of the more staid Scottish preachers as under him. Whitefield was cautious in his assessment of the unusual experiences, and understood the phenomena as 'extraordinary things, proceeding generally from soul-distress.'[75]

The role of Whitefield was very much the guest preacher in the Scottish revival, who was summoned to lend a valuable hand, as well as add his testimony as one who, although young, had witnessed these types of things before. In the face of criticism, this external validation was important. But the revivals at Kilsyth and Cambuslang were primarily parish-based community events, led by the spiritual leaders of those communities, even though they attracted some hearers from across parish boundaries. Whitefield brought an international dimension, but the local leadership remained paramount. The experience of conversion within a defined community, where pastors and people together participated closely in events was common to Northampton, Massachusetts, as well as Kilsyth and Cambuslang. In close-knit, semi-rural communities, for religious experience to be

---

[73] D. MacCulloch, *A History of Christianity*, (London: Allen Lane, 2009), pp 758-759.
[74] Alexander Webster of Edinburgh, quoted in D. Macfarlan, *Revivals of the Eighteenth Century*, pp 76-77.
[75] Whitefield, *Works*, Vol. IV, p 160.

understood and accepted it required validation by the wider community, and especially the local minister as the community leader. This was further affirmed by ministers from the wider region: M'Culloch records twenty-four other ministers as present on the last day of the communion season in 1742.[76]

It has been noted that often the most intense moments of revival in Scotland took place at communion seasons overseen by ministers of the established Church of Scotland.[77] These were important community events replete with social as well as spiritual significance, only held several times each year. Here again Whitefield encountered a pattern different to Anglican usage, but adapted so well to the context that he was invited to become a participant in administering the ordinance. Nonetheless, the role played as an Episcopalian by his 'foul, prelatic, sectarian hands' in the administration of the Presbyterian sacraments did not escape the censure of his bitterest critics.[78]

A key measure of whether the preaching was simply 'dramatic performance', and the response simply 'emotional havoc,' is the degree of permanence of the work. Writing to Robe nine years after Whitefield's visit in 1742, M'Culloch noted 400 converts who were still strong and professing the faith, believing 'in a good measure as becometh the gospel.' Those once renowned as drunkards or cursers who had been reformed through the work of the revival had remained reformed. All were diligent in attendance at 'public ordinances', and in charity and 'public spiritedness.'[79] This work was not just confined to Kilsyth and Cambuslang. Up to a dozen other nearby parishes were reported as seeing large numbers of conversions, or 'persons awakened,' in 1742. The ability of Whitefield and his Scottish friends to 'major on the majors' was central to this: to emphasise the authority of the Bible, to speak of a God who can be personally known and experienced through Jesus Christ, to stress the centrality of justification by faith through God's grace alone, to preach for conversion to Christ on every occasion, and to work together in warm-hearted fellowship

---

[76] McCulloch, 'An Account of the Second Sacrament at Cambuslang', in Robe, *Narrative* (1751 edn), p 35.
[77] See L. Schmidt, *Holy Fairs, Scottish Communions and American Revivals in the Early Modern Period*, (Princeton: Princeton University Press, 1989).
[78] 'The Declaration of the True Presbyterians within the Kingdom of Scotland, Concerning Mr George Whitefield and the Work at Cambuslang, August, 1742', in Tyerman, *Whitefield*, Vol. 2, p 42.
[79] Robe, *Narrative* (1751 edn), pp 308, 313.

with others across the denominations. The emotional experiences came, and went. The revival peaked and passed. But the converts, born-again in such dramatic times and sustained by such clear preaching, proved lasting and genuine.

6.8. Sources

Bebbington, David. *Evangelicalism in Modern Britain: A History from the 1730s to the 1980s.* London: Unwin Hyman, 1989.

Chauncy, C. *Seasonable Thoughts on the State of Religion in New England: A Treatise in Five Parts.* Boston, Rogers and Fowle for Samuel Eliot, 1743.

Dallimore, Arnold. *George Whitefield: The Life and Times of the Great Evangelist of the Eighteenth-Century Revival.* Edinburgh: Banner of Truth, 1970. Vol. 1.

Edwards, Jonathan. *An Humble Attempt to Promote Explicit Agreement and Visible Union of God's People in Extraordinary Prayer,* 1747, in *Works of Jonathan Edwards,* 1834. Edinburgh: Banner of Truth, 1974, Vol. II.

_____. *Select Works of Jonathan Edwards,* Volume 3, *The Religious Affections* (1746) repr. London, Banner of Truth, 1961.

Fawcett, A. *The Cambuslang Revival: The Scottish Evangelical Revival of the Eighteenth Century.* Edinburgh: Banner of Truth, 1971.

Finney, Charles. *Revivals of Religion: Lectures by Charles Grandison Finney,* W.H. Harding (ed.). London: n.p., 1868.

Gillies, J. *Memoirs of the late Reverend George Whitefield.* London: T. Williams, 1812.

Hindmarsh, B. *The Evangelical Conversion Narrative: Spiritual Autobiography in Early Modern England.* Oxford, Oxford University Press, 2005.

MacCulloch, D. *A History of Christianity.* London: Allen Lane, 2009.

Martin, Roger H. *Evangelicals United: Ecumenical Stirrings in Pre-Victorian Britain, 1795-1830,* Studies in Evangelicalism 4. London: Scarecrow Press, 1983.

MacFarlan, D. *The Revivals of the Eighteenth Century Particularly at Cambuslang.* John Johnstone, Edinburgh, n.d.

M'Culloch, W. "Examinations of persons Under Spiritual Concern at Cambuslang, during the Revival in 17-41-42, by Revd. Wm M'Culloch Minister of Cambuslang with Marginal notes by Dr Webster and other ministers". Unpublished Manuscript, New College, University of Edinburgh.

Moody, J. *The God-Centred Life: Insights from Jonathan Edwards for Today.* Leicester: IVP, 2006.

Robe, J. *A Faithful Narrative of the Extraordinary Work of the Spirit of God at Kilsyth and Other Congregations in the Neighbourhood.* Glasgow: n.p., 1789.

_____. *Narrative of the Extraordinary Work of the Spirit of God at Cambuslang, Kilsyth, etc. begun 1742.* Written by J. Robe and others. With attestations by ministers, preachers, etc. Glasgow, 1751. reprint W. Collins: Glasgow, 1840.

_____. *A Short Account of the Remarkable Conversions at Cambuslang*. Glasgow: n.p., 1742.

_____. *Faithful Narrative of Kilsyth*. London: S. Mason, 1742.

Shaw, I.J. *The Greatest is Charity: Andrew Reed (1787-1862), Preacher and Philanthropist*. Darlington: Evangelical Press, 2005.

Schmidt, L. *Holy Fairs, Scottish Communions and American Revivals in the Early Modern Period*. Princeton: Princeton University Press, 1989.

Shaw, Mark. *Global Awakening: How Twentieth Century Revivals Triggered a Christian Revolution* (Downers Grove: IVP, 2010).

Smout, T.C. 'Born Again At Cambuslang: New Evidence On Popular Religion And Literacy In Eighteenth-Century Scotland', *Past and Present* (1982) 97 (1): pp. 114-127.

Stewart, K. and M. Haykin (eds.), M. *The Emergence of Evangelicalism*. Leicester: IVP, 2008.

Stout, H. *The Divine Dramatist: George Whitefield and the Rise of Modern Evangelicalism*. Grand Rapids: Eerdmans, 1991.

Sweeney, D. *The American Evangelical Story*. Grand Rapids: Baker, 2005.

Ward, W.R. *The Protestant Evangelical Awakening*. Cambridge: Cambridge University Press, 1992.

Tyerman, L. *The Life of the Rev. George Whitefield*. London, Hodder and Stoughton, 1876. Vol. 1.

Whitefield, George. 'Letter 337, to Mr. J___ C___, 1 August, 1741', in *Works of George Whitefield*, Vol. 1. London: E&C Dilly, 1771.

_____. The Lord Our Righteousness,' A Sermon Preached on Friday Forenoon, September 11th 1741, in the High Church Yard of Glasgow', in *Works of Whitefield*, Vol. 5.

_____. 'Letter 429 to Rev. Mr. W___, of Dundee, 7 July 1742,' in *Works of Whitefield*, Vol. 1, p. 406.

_____. *Journals of George Whitefield 1737-1745*, 1st edn., reproduced. Oswestry: Quinta Press, 2009.

_____. *Eighteen Sermons*. London: W. Gurney, 1771.

The Genius of George Whitefield

7. The Meeting of Jonathan Edwards and George Whitefield
by Adriaan C. Neele

The sower series reveals that Edwards harbored a deep ambivalence about Whitefield's ministry...[1]

7.1. Introduction

Thus, Ava Chamberlain in a study of Edwards' homilies on the Matthean Parable of the Sower and the Seed – a discourse of six sermons delivered by Edwards a week after Whitefield had preached at his pulpit at Northampton on October 17, 1740.[2] Jonathan Edwards' (1703-58) ambivalence about the ministry of the British evangelist, according to Chamberlain,

> was rooted theologically in his conviction that Whitefield's theatrical preaching style dangerously encouraged religious hypocrisy, and personally, in feelings of professional rivalry.[3]

This assertion is echoed by George Marsden noting that Edwards 'was uneasy with some of Whitefield's style and cautioned against being distracted by mere "eloquence," "aptness of expression," and "beautiful gestures."'[4] Scholars have pointed to the Sower-series as an indication that Edwards was uncomfortable with some of the effects of Whitefield's preaching – problematic 'sudden' conversions, 'self-flattering hopes,' and 'superficial impressions' – and perhaps even jealous of his success, especially in light of what Edwards felt to be the barrenness of his ministry during the late 1730s.[5] Hence, Kimnach's notion of Edwards' 'skepticism of the efficacy of Whitefield's

---

[1] Ava Chamberlain, 'The Grand Sower of the Seed: Jonathan Edward's Critique of George Whitefield,' *The New England Quarterly*, Vol. 70. No. 3 (1997), p 384.
[2] Jonathan Edwards, 'Divine Husbandman (On the Parable of the Sower and the Seed),' in Kenneth P. Minkema and Adriaan C. Neele (eds.) *Sermons by Jonathan Edwards on the Matthean Parables*, Vol. II, (Eugene, OR: Cascade Books, 2012).
[3] Chamberlain, 'The Grand Sower of the Seed,' p 384.
[4] George Marsden, *Jonathan Edwards: A Life* (New Haven: Yale University Press, 2003), p 212.
[5] Chamberlain, 'The Grand Sower of the Seed,' p 372.

preaching,'6 and Pettit's observation of 'Edwards' reaction against the extremes of Whitefield and other early revival preachers,'7 suggesting moreover, 'Edwards was not a close friend of Whitefield.'8

On the one hand, these scholarly assessments may have merit considering the time Edwards was associated with Whitefield in public – a post-Great Awakening setting and putting Northampton's pastor in a delicate position. When Whitefield's second preaching tour in the colonies was announced in 1744, his opponents worked to insure a cold reception and to spread animosity towards him. Thomas Clap (1703-1767), Rector of Yale College, which had denounced Whitefield, declared in print that Whitefield had claimed that he was going to replace the unconverted clergy of New England with young ministers from England, Scotland, and Ireland. What is more, Clap claimed he was quoting from private letters by Edwards as his authority. In response, Edwards categorically denied ever having talked with Whitefield about such a plan, and continued to be a vocal supporter of Whitefield and of the revivals. But he did describe the substance of some of his conversations with Whitefield, which also has some bearing on the content of the sermons on the parable of the sower and the seed. Edwards wrote, following Whitefield's first visit to New England:

> I indeed have told several persons, that I once purposely took an opportunity to talk with Mr. Whitefield alone about impulses…that I told him some reasons I had to think he gave too great heed to such things: and have told what manner of replies he made; and what reasons I offered against such things. And I also said that Mr. Whitefield did not seem to be offended with me: but yet did not seem to be inclined to have a great deal of discourse about it: and that in the time of it he did not appear to be convinced by anything I said… It is also true… that I thought Mr. Whitefield liked me not so well….9

---

[6] *The Works of Jonathan Edwards* (New Haven: Yale University Press, 1957-2008), Vol. 25 p 7. Hereafter *WJE* Vol.: page no.
[7] *WJE* Vol. 7 p 9.
[8] *WJE* Vol 7 p 38.
[9] Jonathan Edwards, *Copies of Two Letters Cited by the Reverend Mr. Clap* (Boston, 1745), pp 6-7, '…for my opposing these things: and though he treated me with great kindness; yet he never made so much of an intimate of me, as of some others. It is also true, that I once talked with Mr. Whitefield (though not alone) about judging other persons to be unconverted.' Rev. Jonathan Barber, minister of Orient, Long Island, New York, 1735-40.

For Edwards' earliest biographer, Perry Miller, reason enough to conclude, and probably at the expense of Whitefield, '[W]ithin the fold of revivalism, there are no personalities more uncongenial than Whitefield and Edwards.'[10]

7.2. Edwards and Whitefield: Background

Although Edwards deleted a passage of Brainerd's admiration for Whitefield in the editing of *Life of David Brainerd*[11]—a practice that was continued by Edward's great-grandson Sereno Dwight (1786-1850) who edited-out Edwards' praise for Whitefield in a sermon published as *Charity and its Fruits*,[12] the question must be raised: had Edwards always been 'ambivalent' to Whitefield's ministry?

Leading up to the Evangelist's meeting with Edwards in October 1740, the first explicit reference to Whitefield in the surviving Edwards corpus appears in the sermon *God's Grace Carried On in Other Places* of December, 1739:

> But he that has been most taken notice of, of whose success we have the greatest fame, is Mr. Whitefield. [He is a] young man [who is] a minister of the Church of England, who labors obediently [and] insists very much on the doctrines of faith in Christ and the New Birth.[13]

In February 1740, following, Edwards wrote to the young and energetic preacher in England:

> My request to you is that, in your intended journey through New England the next summer, you would be pleased to visit

---

[10] Miller, *Jonathan Edwards*, pp 133, 142-43.
[11] *WJE* Vol. 7 p 149. David Brainerd, 'About this time it was a great comfort to me that the Rev. Mr. Whitefield came through the land though I had not the opportunity to see and hear him, yet hearing by others of his doctrines and conduct my soul was refreshed and seemed knit to him...'
[12] *WJE* Vol. 8 p 757. *Charity and its Fruits*, 'Concerning "particular characters" that are distinguishing of degrees of excellence, a Christian should seek those experiences that are more attended with the greatest exercises of humility; those attended with the greatest self-denial. The copy continues: "This as the Rev. Mr. Whitefield says in one of his sermons is the grand secret of Christianity, the great secret of being a real Christian seems to lie very much here'— edited out by Dwight. This reference to a published sermon of Whitefield is one reason for dating JE's sermon on 1 Corinthians 12:31 later than the *Charity* series.
[13] *WJE* Vol. 22 p 108.

Northampton. I hope it is not wholly from curiosity that I desire to see and hear you in this place; but I apprehend, from what I have heard, that you are one that has the blessing of heaven attending you wherever you go; and I have a great desire...that such a blessing as attends your person and labors may descend on this town, and may enter mine own house...[14]

Edwards' expectation of the Grand Itinerant was heightened writing to Josiah Willard, Secretary of the Province of Massachusetts, June 1, 1740:

From what we hear of the Reverend Mr. [George] Whitefield, his great labors and success...I cannot but hope that God is about to accomplish glorious things for his church...Mr. Whitefield has been so kind as to send me his Journals, which give me a considerable idea of the hopeful state of reviving religion in England.[15]

In August of that year Edwards even mentioned Whitefield by name in the sermon *Children Ought to Love the Lord Jesus Christ Above All*:

And consider further, to stir you, how many have truly loved Christ while they are young. And on this occasion I will tell you what account the Rev. Mr. Whitefield has given me in a letter that I received from him this week past – the minister that you have doubtless heard of, that has had such great success in many places.[16]

Last but not least, a week before Whitefield's arrival Edwards conveyed to the Connecticut minister Eleazar Wheelock,

And particularly should be earnest with God that he would still uphold, and succeed the Reverend Mr. [George] Whitefield, the instrument that it has pleased him to improve to do such great things for the honor of his name...[17]

---

[14] *WJE* Vol. 16 p 87.
[15] *WJE* Vol. 16 pp 82-83.
[16] *WJE* Vol. 22 p 107. See fn. 2, 'JE leaves several blank lines in the MS to indicate where to read the letter, which has not been located. We may get some idea of what Whitefield wrote by looking at what he said about children in his Journals. In October 1740, for example, while in Boston, upon hearing of a sickly child who died before he could hear Whitefield preach, the Grand Itinerant was encouraged to "speak to little ones.... "Little children, if your parents will not come to Christ, do you come, and go to heaven without them."' (*George Whitefield's Journals* [London: Banner of Truth Trust, 1960], p 469).
[17] *WJE* Vol. 16 p 84.

Edwards' biographer George Marsden writes,

> just as the light from Northampton seemed to be receding, Edwards expectantly awaited George Whitefield's coming to Northampton to see if the evangelist could bring the light back.[18]

7.3. Edwards and Whitefield: Meeting

And so, amidst Edwards' family life, church affairs and correspondence, and preaching, then, Whitefield arrived at Northampton in October 1740. Edwards' life was provincial, but he had an international horizon. Whitefield – the 'divine dramatist'[19] – appeared in the hinterlands of New England having just completed a successful and major preaching campaign at Boston, New England's urban capital, but bringing a trans-Atlantic experience. 'Contrasting co-workers' is the phrase that comes to mind when envisioning these two preachers in the parsonage in Northampton: Whitefield, the dynamic, ambitious, entrepreneurial awakener, and Edwards with his structured, scrupulously careful, and aristocratic air. And yet, both the twenty-five-year-old Grand Itinerant[20] and the author of *A Faithful Narrative*, twelve years his senior, spent most of their lives preparing and preaching sermons.

Whitefield's five addresses to the congregation and to private assemblies from October 17-19 were moving, rejuvenating, and inspiring. From Edwards' perspective, writing later to Thomas Prince:

> [H]e {Whitefield} preached here four sermons in the meetinghouse (besides a private lecture at my house), one on Friday, another on Saturday, and two upon the sabbath. The congregation was extraordinarily melted by every sermon; almost the whole assembly being in tears for a great part of sermon time.[21]

While Whitefield recorded in his Journal a similar point of view:

> Good Mr. Edwards wept during the whole time of exercise. The people were equally affected; and, in the afternoon, the power

---

[18] Marsden, *Jonathan Edwards: A Life*, p 202.
[19] Harry S. Stout, *The Divine Dramatist: George Whitefield and the Rise of Modern Evangelism* (Grand Rapids: Eerdmans, 2001).
[20] Harry S. Stout, *The New England Soul: Preaching and Religious Culture in Colonial New England* (Oxford: Oxford University Press, 1986), p 189.
[21] *WJE* Vol. 16 p 116.

increased yet more...[22]

It was like the revival of 1734-35 all over again – a return Edwards had been seeking for five years. But while the parishioners of Northampton and beyond were stirred anew, Whitefield was not appreciated by all New England religious leaders. Some of the pastors refused to admit him into their pulpits; others were simply puzzled by him. Daniel Wadsworth of Hartford, for example, recorded in his diary for October 6 that he read a description of the 'wonders wro't' by Whitefield's preaching in Boston – 'but alas,' he queried, 'what are they?'[23]

On the one hand, Edwards 'once purposely took an opportunity to talk with Mr. Whitefield alone about impulses,'[24] but on the other hand, Edwards was genuinely impressed with Whitefield as an instrument of God, writing to him, 'God seems to have succeeded your labors amongst us.'[25] We do not know that Edwards had any knowledge of his famous visitor's own assessment of his preaching surrounding his visit at Northampton. Whitefield wrote in his journal that his experience there gave him 'an affecting Prospect of the Glories of the upper World, ... as if a Time of Refreshing was come.'[26]

7.4. *Edwards and Whitefield: Hearing of the Word*

Nonetheless, Edwards saw the need to do an extended assessment of Whitefield and the emotions he had raised. He commenced in November his series on Matthew 13:3-7, entitled *Divine Husbandmen* dealing in detail with the efficacy of the Word – and with Whitefield's recent preaching no doubt in mind.

In the third sermon, for example, Edwards considers the stony ground. He describes this sort of ground, how seeds grow in it, and what becomes of the growth. His Proposition: 'The hearts of some of

---

[22] George Whitefield, *A Continuation of the Reverend Mr. Whitefield's Journal, from a few days after his arrival at Savannah, June the fourth, to his leaving Stanford, the last town in New-England, October 29, 1740* (Philadelphia, 1740), p 108. See also, Arnold A. Dallimore, *George Whitefield: The Life and Times of the Great Evangelist of the Eighteenth-Century Revival* (2 vols. Westchester, Ill., Cornerstone Books, 1971), Vol. 1 p 539; *WJE* Vol. 4 p 545.
[23] *Diary of Daniel Wadsworth* (Hartford, 1894), p 55.
[24] *WJE* Vol. 16 p 157.
[25] *WJE* Vol. 16 p 87.
[26] Whitefield, *A Continuation of the Reverend Mr. Whitefield's Journal*, pp 106-7.

the hearers of the Word preached, are like a rock with a thin covering of earth.' He notices first how hearers' minds may be 'impressed and affected,' in that they may have 'a sort of belief' in what they hear – assent to the doctrines, assent to the truth of the Word, and conviction – but it is temporary. Providing a number of apparent allusions to Whitefield's preaching style and its effects on auditors, Edwards points out that stony-ground hearers may even have initial joy in hearing the Word, but their joy arises from pleasure in the manner of preaching, being taken with the eloquence, fervency, and gestures of the speaker rather than having 'joy in the things preached.'

Likewise, Sermon Four treats v. 5 of the chapter, with the Proposition, 'Sudden conversions are very often false,' a statement that seems to arise from Edwards' fear that many in Northampton claiming conversion upon hearing Whitefield may be the victims of fleeting emotions. Edwards does not deny the reality of sudden and unexpected conversion, since the Bible has several notable instances of it. Ordinarily, however – a point Edwards makes in numerous regular sermons – God works in a gradual method over time.

In the sixth and final sermon Edwards considers v. 7, on the 'thorny ground.' The soil of the hearts of some hearers has never been plowed, and so is full of 'useless growth,' that is, ruled by a 'carnal spirit' and the 'natural produce of the heart.' Thorny-ground hearers can 'show considerable regard to the Word of God for a while, yet these thorns do at length prevail and choke the Word, so that it never brings forth any saving fruit.' This, unfortunately, was something that Edwards had seen too often among his own congregants. So, in the new round of awakenings caused by Whitefield's arrival, Edwards was asking: Will the thorns quickly grow back again in the soil that the sower has sown?

As this succinct review of *Divine Husbandmen* reveals, Edwards was a preacher concerned with his listeners' self-discernment, apprehensive about the reception of his sermons, and whether they would have a lasting effect.

But so was Whitefield.

And here, one needs to re-evaluate Edwards' 'deep ambivalence' concerning Whitefield's ministry – an interpretation mainly based on the reading of Edwards' *Divine Husbandmen* or Matthean Parable of the Sower and Seed sermon series, and Whitefield's second visit to New England. For this reassessment I offer two considerations.

First, a rather unknown sermon of Whitefield needs to be read, and secondly, an overlooked private lecture of Edwards needs to be taken into account.

In 1739 Whitefield preached *Directions How to Hear Sermons*, based on Luke 8:18, in London. The address, published that same year, revealed a preacher concerned with making sure his hearers received every benefit from preaching that they could. What is more, the address drew on a familiar topic: the parable of the sower. At the outset of the sermon, Whitefield asserts, 'The Occasion of our Lord's giving this Caution ... under the Similitude of a Sower' was to intimate 'how few there were amongst them who would receive any saving benefit from his Doctrine, or bring forth Fruit unto Perfection.'[27]

The discourse presents two main thoughts. First, Whitefield shows that God sends ministers who preach the gospel, and listeners, consequently, are obliged to hear them. Throughout history 'God has constantly separated to himself a certain order of men to preach,'[28] and though many thousands hear sermons, only a 'few [hearers], comparatively speaking, are effectually influenced by them.' Therefore, Whitefield warns, 'take heed how you hear.' Furthermore, the British itinerant provides 'cautions and directions' for hearing the gospel with 'profit and advantage,' including bringing forth fruit, or putting in practice what has been heard. Whitefield's sermon subsequently crossed the Atlantic and was reprinted in 1740 at Philadelphia and in a third edition at Boston, probably in part to prepare the way for his colony tour later that year.

Secondly, and most likely immediately after Whitefield's time in Northampton, yet preceding the discourses on the parable of the sower, Edwards delivered a brief – but significant for the circumstances – sermon or private lecture on 2 Corinthians 2:15-16, with the doctrine, 'Gospel ministers a savor of life or of death.' He opened the sermon by asserting that 'the Apostle [Paul] was the most eminent minister of the gospel. He preached in many places. Above all others, [he was] the most remarkable for his success.' Perhaps Northampton's pastor was referring indirectly to the British evangelist when he noted that 'his success was not alike in all places, amongst all sorts of people, nor with different persons in the same places and among the same sort of people.' Edwards proposes (or, reflecting on his recent failure as an

---

[27] George Whitefield, *Directions How to Hear Sermons* (London, 1739), p 1.
[28] Whitefield, *Directions*, p 4.

awakener, comforts himself with) the thought that 'ministers that faithfully preach the gospel of Christ are accepted of God, and are as a sweet savor to him, whether they are successful or no.' He also warns his hearers not to reject gospel preaching: 'It is especially thus when God sends a messenger that is eminent.' Edwards may have had Whitefield in mind in these words, as well as when he offers several observations on 'the eloquence of the preacher, the fervency of preaching, beautiful gestures, a becoming, beautiful manner of address' – attributes that the more staid, traditional Edwards lacked. In closing, Edwards applies the Scripture with a call for self-examination 'whether the gospel of Christ has been a savor unto life' or not. Persons may be 'very variously affected' with the preaching, and 'yet not have it thus as a sweet savor.'[29] Furthermore, he encourages his hearers

> to be in good earnest in making a good improvement of the late labors of that servant of God, whom God has sent to us from afar, that it may be effectual for our great good and not for our great hurt. Let us consider how we have backslidden. How rare [are] conversions, [how] rare convictions. This seems to have been what he chiefly aimed at—to stir us.[30]

Comparing, then, Whitefield's *Directions How to Hear Sermons* and Edwards on 2 Corinthians 2:15-16 and the *Sower Discourse*, the question arises: did Edwards read Whitefield's *Directions*? The similar thoughts of these preachers on preaching (and hearing), and their use of similar Scripture proofs, would indicate that he did. In these pieces, both Whitefield and Edwards discuss the duty of ministers to preach the gospel faithfully and of listeners to attend their message in a becoming manner. Whitefield asserts, 'people are obliged to attend'[31] to the minister's preaching because 'there have always been particular persons set apart by God to instruct and exhort his people.' Likewise, Edwards states that when a gospel preacher 'comes to a people, either as being regularly called to office among them as their settled pastor, or is providentially sent among them, they ought be looked upon as sent by the owner of the field of the world,' that is, God.[32] As Whitefield notes that it is the 'duty of ministers to preach (and woe be unto them if they

---

[29] *WJE* Vol. 22 pp 205, 207, 208.
[30] *WJE* Vol. 22 p 209.
[31] Whitefield, *Directions*, p 5.
[32] Edwards, *Divine Husbandman*, p 33.

do not preach the gospel, for a necessity is laid upon them),'[33] so Edwards comments, 'Ministers can but deliver their message.'[34] These are all fairly common contemporary sentiments about preaching, but when we look closer, we see even more parallels. Whitefield's overarching concern in his *Directions* is the hearer's response. He 'proves' from various Scripture passages 'that everyone ought to take the opportunity of hearing sermons.'[35] If there are those who refuse 'to attend to so great a means of their salvation,' Whitefield asserts with exclamatory rhetoric, 'How much more tolerable will it be for Tyre and Sidon, for Sodom and Gomorrah, than for such sinners?' Edwards shares a similar concern for his hearers, and employs also Sodom and Gomorrah for comparative purpose. In his attempt to awaken 'sinners of this congregation,' he even delivers one of the most confrontational statements to be found in all of his sermons:

> How loud have been the calls of God's Word, and also of his minister to you. If I were to choose the place where I would preach with the greatest probability of success, and Sodom was now standing, I had rather go into Sodom and preach to the men of Sodom than preach to you – and should have a great deal more hopes of success.[36]

Following Whitefield as well as Jesus' own word in Scripture, Edwards actually outdoes Whitefield in this ultimatum to his congregation.

In addition, Whitefield cautions his hearers not to listen to a preacher out of curiosity, out of formality or hypocrisy: instead, he counsels them 'to give diligent heed ... whilst you are hearing the Word of God.' As hearers in Christ's time were obliged to hear him, so Whitefield asserts that modern audiences of gospel preachers 'should hang upon them to hear their words.' Moreover, he cautions against entertaining any prejudice against ministers, not to depend too much on the preacher, or 'to think more highly of him than you ought to think.' Whitefield is aware that people prefer 'one teacher in opposition to another.' But he rhetorically asks his audience, 'Are not all ministers sent forth to be ministering ambassadors ... are they not all therefore greatly to be esteemed for their work's sake?' For Whitefield, to prefer one minister at the expense of another is 'earthly, sensual, devilish.'

---

[33] Whitefield, *Directions*, p 5.
[34] Edwards, *Divine Husbandman*, p 36.
[35] Whitefield, *Directions*, p 3.
[36] Edwards, *Divine Husbandman*, p 49.

Furthermore, the success of the gospel is not because of the preacher; 'Christ has promised to be with his ministers.' If their labours are ineffectual, it is because congregations 'are not prepared to receive them.' Though 'God's ordinary way of acting [is] ... to visit those with the Power of his Word, who humbly wait ... it does indeed sometimes happen [that] ... a sinner is forcibly work'd upon by a publick Sermon, and pluck'd as a Firebrand out of the Fire.' Finally, he cautions his hearers not to consider popularity or applause of the preacher: such motives, according to the Grand Itinerant, are 'exceedingly dangerous.'[37] In his discourse on the sower, Edwards expressed admonitions similar to those of Whitefield in his *Directions*. Edwards distinguishes 'hypocrites' and 'false professors' from sincere believers.[38] 'God expects a better reception and improvement of his means from us than from others,' he asserts, 'for we have received much more than others.'[39]

Moreover, for Edwards, as for Whitefield, his listeners may prefer certain preachers. Ministers of the Word may be either 'regularly called to office' or 'providentially sent among them,' but, as Edwards proposes in his sermon on 2 Corinthians 2:15-16, 'Those ministers that faithfully preach the gospel of Christ are accepted of God, and are as a sweet savor to him, whether they are successful or no.'[40] Though sudden conversions may happen, they may be also false. Echoing Whitefield, Northampton's pastor confirms that 'True conversion ordinarily is not suddenly wrought; commonly, some considerable time is taken up after persons begin to be awakened before they are thoroughly brought home to Christ.'[41]

Furthermore, Edwards notes that if the preacher's labours should be ineffectual, it is not because of the gospel but because of 'our past backslidings, and the dreadful consequences of them.'[42]

Finally, Edwards, like Whitefield in his *Directions*, warns his people not to be greatly pleased with the 'aptness of expression,' such as 'the eloquence of the preacher, fervency, beautiful manner of address, and filled with admiration.'[43] Such hearers, according to Edwards – echoing Whitefield's warning not 'to admire the oratory ... only out of curiosity' –

---

[37] Whitefield, *Directions*, pp 9, 12, 16, 13.
[38] Edwards, *Divine Husbandman*, pp 60 ff., 82ff.
[39] *WJE* Vol. 22 p 209.
[40] *WJE* Vol. 22 p 206.
[41] See below.
[42] *WJE* Vol. 22 p 210
[43] *WJE* Vol. 22 p 208.

are in danger as long as the gospel of Christ is not a sweet savour to them. 'But fear not, you little flock,' Whitefield concludes: 'those who receive the word with meekness will 'bring forth the peaceable fruits of righteousness.'[44] Edwards' conclusion, however, comes down to three questions: 'Do you receive it as a savor of life, with a firm faith in Christ as a living Savior?' 'Does the effect abide?' 'Does it bring forth fruit?' 'This,' Edwards closes, 'we find to be the main distinction between [profitable hearers and others] in the parable of the sower and the seed.'

7.5. Conclusion

Whitefield's meeting with Edwards in 1740, then, shows that the latter had more in common with and was more appreciative of the British Itinerant than is often suggested – an assessment supported by Edwards' encouraging report to Whitefield written immediately following the completion of the discourse on the sower. Edwards wrote in December of that year, which was excerpted in a London evangelical journal under the title, 'An Account of the most Remarkable Particulars relating to the present progress of the Gospel':

> I have joyful tidings to send you concerning the state of religion in this place. It has been gradually reviving and prevailing more and more, ever since you was here. Religion is become abundantly more the subject of conversation; other things that seemed to impede it, are for the present laid aside. I have reason to think that a considerable number of our young people, some of them children, have already been savingly brought home to Christ. I hope salvation has come to this house since you was in it, with respect to one, if not more, of my children. The Spirit of God seems to be at work with others of the family. That blessed work seems now to be going on in this place, especially amongst those that are young. And as God seems to have succeeded your labors amongst us, and prayers for us, I desire your fervent prayers for us may yet be continued, that God would not be to us as a wayfaring man, that turns aside to tarry but for a night, but that he would more and more pour out his Spirit upon us, and no more depart from us; and for me in particular, that I may be filled with his Spirit, and may become fervent, as a flame of fire in my work, and may be abundantly

---

[44] Whitefield, *Directions*, p 17.

succeeded, and that it would please God...[45]

In conclusion, Edwards was less ambivalent to Whitefield's ministry during his first meeting at Northampton. Moreover, that visit had another unexpected result in Edwards' preaching – Edwards is clearly moving his fully written out sermons toward an outline style that allowed greater room for 'freedom' in the pulpit.[46]

Meanwhile, back in England, as Whitefield's biographer Harry Stout remarks, popular publications, such as 'The Weekly Miscellany' censured Whitefield's style as dangerously 'enthusiastic.'[47] But it was Whitefield who warned his audience in *Directions how to hear Sermons* 'not to admire the oratory ... only out of curiosity.'[48] Thus, Edwards was not the first who expressed his concern about Whitefield's preaching style; ironically Whitefield himself had done so previously. Unfortunately, his warnings went unheeded by many in the ferment of revival. Edwards' invitation to Whitefield to come to Northampton in 1740 had many repercussions, giving rise to much discussion – for Edwards, Whitefield, their contemporaries, and modern interpreters. The main, and often forgotten, concern for both sowers of the seed was the advancement of God's kingdom. Furthermore, their preaching produced fruit. By the spring of 1741, with moving experiences and a massive impact on the American scene, the Great Awakening was in full swing in New England and would spread elsewhere.

7.6. Sources

Chamberlain, A. "The Grand Sower of the Seed: Jonathan Edward's Critique of George Whitefield," *The New England Quarterly*, Vol. 70. No. 3 (1997).

Dallimore, Arnold A. *George Whitefield: The Life and Times of the Great Evangelist of the Eighteenth-Century Revival*. Westchester, Ill., Cornerstone Books, 1971.

Edwards, Jonathan. *Copies of Two Letters Cited by the Reverend Mr. Clap*. Boston, 1745.

———. *The Works of Jonathan Edwards* (New Haven: Yale University Press, 1957-2008).

———. *Divine Husbandman (On the Parable of the Sower and the Seed), Sermons by Jonathan Edwards on the Matthean Parables*, Vol. II, Kenneth P. Minkema, Adriaan C. Neele (eds.). Eugene, OR: Cascade Books, 2012.

---

[45] *The Weekly History: or, An Account of the most Remarkable Particulars relating to the present Progress of the Gospel*, no. 9 (London, 1741), pp 1-2.
[46] *WJE* Vol. 22 p 491.
[47] Stout, *The Divine Dramatist*, p 83.
[48] Whitefield, *Directions*, p 17.

Marsden, George. *Jonathan Edwards: A Life*. New Haven: Yale University Press, 2003.

Miller, Perry. *Jonathan Edwards*. New York: William Sloane Associates, 1949.

Stout, Harry S. *The Divine Dramatist: George Whitefield and the Rise of Modern Evangelism*. Grand Rapids: Eerdmans, 2001.

———. *The New England Soul: Preaching and Religious Culture in Colonial New England*. Oxford: Oxford University Press, 1986.

Wadsworth, D. *Diary of Daniel Wadsworth*. Hartford, 1894.

The Weekly History: or, An Account of the most Remarkable Particulars relating to the present Progress of the Gospel, no. 9. London, 1741.

Whitefield, George. *Directions How to Hear Sermons*. London, 1739.

———. *A Continuation of the Reverend Mr. Whitefield's Journal, from a few days after his arrival at Savannah, June the fourth, to his leaving Stanford, the last town in New-England, October 29, 1740*. Philadelphia, 1740.

———. *George Whitefield's Journals* (London: Banner of Truth Trust, 1960).

8. Conference Closing Prayer
by Ross Anderson

Heavenly Father,

Thank you for your rich blessing on our Whitefield Symposium 2014, and thank you too for blessing this College that we have been able to celebrate our 25th year in this way.

Thank you for our brothers who have addressed us on Whitefield as a Pastor, a Preacher, an Anglican, an Evangelist, an Evangelical, and a Theologian.

Heavenly Father, we bring before you this College – George Whitefield College – and in particular our students. Just as you raised up Whitefield, and in spite of his sin and weakness you chose to use him mightily in the extension of your Kingdom, so we now humbly ask that you will raise up from our midst a new generation of preachers and Bible teachers, who will go into the world and especially into Africa, and give themselves wholeheartedly in your glorious employ.

We pray that from this College here at the bottom end of Africa, you will raise up men and women who are mighty in the Scriptures, whose lives are dominated by a sense of the greatness, the majesty, the holiness of God, and whose minds and hearts are aglow with the doctrines of grace. May they be disciples who have learned what it is to die to self, to human aims and personal ambitions; men and women who are willing to be fools for Christ's sake; who will bear reproach and falsehood, who will labour and suffer, and whose supreme desire will be not to gain earth's accolades but to win the Master's approval when they appear before his final judgment seat.

Heavenly Father, in particular we dare to ask – only in Christ's name, the great Head of the Church, and only for Christ's sake – that you would please raise up for Africa her own band of 'George Whitefields': Men and women who will lead by faithfully and accurately preaching and teaching the Word of God – both the Old Testament and the New. Men and women who will speak with broken hearts and tear-filled eyes, and upon whose announcement of the Gospel you will grant an extraordinary effusion of the Holy Spirit, and who will witness the regeneration and transformation into the image of Christ thousands upon thousands of Africa's people.

Our Heavenly Father, you who made a covenant with Abraham and Isaac and Jacob to bless the nations of the world, you who gave your only Son to fulfil that covenant, you who will consummate your great and eternal Kingdom at his *parousia*, please, O Lord our God, raise up 'George Whitefields' for South Africa, for Lesotho and Swaziland, for Mozambique, Zimbabwe, and Namibia. For Angola, Zambia and Malawi. For all of Africa, from Mauritania in the West, to Ethiopia in the East; from Libya in the North, to Botswana on our border.

Heavenly Father, please would you use this College toward the raising up of such preachers, evangelists, and ministers of the Gospel, and toward the granting of a mighty revival such as Africa has never seen, that will turn Africa's heart to you.

We remember, Lord Jesus, the words of your Apostle John:

You are worthy to take the scroll and to open its seals, because you were slain, and with your blood you purchased men for God from every tribe and language and people and nation (Revelation 5:9).

Lord Jesus, remember Africa. Remember Africa, not in judgment but in mercy. Heavenly Father, for Christ's sake, remember Africa and save your people. We ask this in the great and glorious name of our Lord Jesus Christ. And we ask it for His glory.

Amen.[1]

---

[1] This prayer is based in part on: Arnold A. Dallimore, *George Whitefield: The Life and Times of the Great Evangelist of the Eighteenth-Century Revival* (Edinburgh: The Banner of Truth Trust, 1970), pp 15-16; and Stephen Mansfield, *Forgotten Founding Father: The Heroic Legacy of George Whitefield* (Nashville, TN: Highland Books), pp 214-215.

If you have enjoyed this book, you might like to consider

- *supporting the work of the Latimer Trust*
- *reading more of our publications*
- *recommending them to others*

See www.latimertrust.org for more information.

Latimer Publications

Latimer Studies

LS 01	The Evangelical Anglican Identity Problem	Jim Packer
LS 02	The ASB Rite A Communion: A Way Forward	Roger Beckwith
LS 03	The Doctrine of Justification in the Church of England	Robin Leaver
LS 04	Justification Today: The Roman Catholic and Anglican Debate	R. G. England
LS 05/06	Homosexuals in the Christian Fellowship	David Atkinson
LS 07	Nationhood: A Christian Perspective	O. R. Johnston
LS 08	Evangelical Anglican Identity: Problems and Prospects	Tom Wright
LS 09	Confessing the Faith in the Church of England Today	Roger Beckwith
LS 10	A Kind of Noah's Ark? The Anglican Commitment to Comprehensiveness	Jim Packer
LS 11	Sickness and Healing in the Church	Donald Allister
LS 12	Rome and Reformation Today: How Luther Speaks to the New Situation	James Atkinson
LS 13	Music as Preaching: Bach, Passions and Music in Worship	Robin Leaver
LS 14	Jesus Through Other Eyes: Christology in a Multi-faith Context	Christopher Lamb
LS 15	Church and State Under God	James Atkinson,
LS 16	Language and Liturgy	Gerald Bray, Steve Wilcockson, Robin Leaver
LS 17	Christianity and Judaism: New Understanding, New Relationship	James Atkinson
LS 18	Sacraments and Ministry in Ecumenical Perspective	Gerald Bray
LS 19	The Functions of a National Church	Max Warren
LS19 (2nd ed.)	British Values and the National Church: Essays on Church and State from 1964-2014	Ed. David Holloway
LS 20/21	The Thirty-Nine Articles: Their Place and Use Today	Jim Packer, Roger Beckwith
LS 22	How We Got Our Prayer Book	T.W. Drury, Roger Beckwith
LS 23/24	Creation or Evolution: a False Antithesis?	Mike Poole, Gordon Wenham
LS 25	Christianity and the Craft	Gerard Moate
LS 26	ARCIC II and Justification	Alister McGrath
LS 27	The Challenge of the Housechurches	Tony Higton, Gilbert Kirby
LS 28	Communion for Children? The Current Debate	A. A. Langdon
LS 29/30	Theological Politics	Nigel Biggar
LS 31	Eucharistic Consecration in the First Four Centuries and its Implications for Liturgical Reform	Nigel Scotland
LS 32	A Christian Theological Language	Gerald Bray
LS 33	Mission in Unity: The Bible and Missionary Structures	Duncan McMann
LS 34	Stewards of Creation: Environmentalism in the Light of Biblical Teaching	Lawrence Osborn
LS 35/36	Mission and Evangelism in Recent Thinking: 1974-1986	Robert Bashford
LS 37	Future Patterns of Episcopacy: Reflections in Retirement	Stuart Blanch
LS 38	Christian Character: Jeremy Taylor and Christian Ethics Today	David Scott
LS 39	Islam: Towards a Christian Assessment	Hugh Goddard
LS 40	Liberal Catholicism: Charles Gore and the Question of Authority	G. F. Grimes
LS 41/42	The Christian Message in a Multi-faith Society	Colin Chapman
LS 43	The Way of Holiness 1: Principles	D. A. Ousley
LS 44/45	The Lambeth Articles	V. C. Miller

Latimer Publications

LS 46	*The Way of Holiness 2: Issues*	D. A. Ousley
LS 47	*Building Multi-Racial Churches*	John Root
LS 48	*Episcopal Oversight: A Case for Reform*	David Holloway
LS 49	*Euthanasia: A Christian Evaluation*	Henk Jochemsen
LS 50/51	*The Rough Places Plain: AEA 1995*	
LS 52	*A Critique of Spirituality*	John Pearce
LS 53/54	*The Toronto Blessing*	Martyn Percy
LS 55	*The Theology of Rowan Williams*	Garry Williams
LS 56/57	*Reforming Forwards? The Process of Reception and the Consecration of Woman as Bishops*	Peter Toon
LS 58	*The Oath of Canonical Obedience*	Gerald Bray
LS 59	*The Parish System: The Same Yesterday, Today And For Ever?*	Mark Burkill
LS 60	*'I Absolve You': Private Confession and the Church of England*	Andrew Atherstone
LS 61	*The Water and the Wine: A Contribution to the Debate on Children and Holy Communion*	Roger Beckwith, Andrew Daunton-Fear
LS 62	*Must God Punish Sin?*	Ben Cooper
LS 63	*Too Big For Words? The Transcendence of God and Finite Human Speech*	Mark D. Thompson
LS 64	*A Step Too Far: An Evangelical Critique of Christian Mysticism*	Marian Raikes
LS 65	*The New Testament and Slavery: Approaches and Implications*	Mark Meynell
LS 66	*The Tragedy of 1662: The Ejection and Persecution of the Puritans*	Lee Gatiss
LS 67	*Heresy, Schism & Apostasy*	Gerald Bray
LS 68	*Paul in 3D: Preaching Paul as Pastor, Story-teller and Sage*	Ben Cooper
LS69	*Christianity and the Tolerance of Liberalism: J.Gresham Machen and the Presbyterian Controversy of 1922-1937*	Lee Gatiss
LS70	*An Anglican Evangelical Identity Crisis: The Churchman–Anvil Affair of 1981-4*	Andrew Atherstone
LS71	*Empty and Evil: The worship of other faiths in 1 Corinthians 8-10 and today*	Rohintan Mody
LS72	*To Plough or to Preach: Mission Strategies in New Zealand during the 1820s*	Malcolm Falloon
LS73	*Plastic People: How Queer Theory is changing us*	Peter Sanlon
LS74	*Deification and Union with Christ: Salvation in Orthodox and Reformed thought*	Slavko Eždenci
LS75	*As It Is Written: Interpreting the Bible with Boldness*	Benjamin Sargent
LS76	*Light From Dark Ages? An Evangelical Critique of Celtic Spirituality*	Marian Raikes
LS77	*The Ethics of Usury*	Ben Cooper
LS78	*For Us and For Our Salvation: 'Limited Atonement' in the Bible, Doctrine, History and Ministry*	Lee Gatiss
LS79	*Positive Complementarianism: The Key Biblical Texts*	Ben Cooper
LS80	*Were they Preaching 'Another Gospel'? Justification by faith in the Second Century*	Andrew Daunton-Fear
LS81	*Thinking Aloud: Responding to the Contemporary Debate about Marriage, Sexuality and Reconciliation*	Martin Davie
LS82	*Spells, Sorcerers and Spirits: Magic and the Occult in the Bible*	Kirsten Birkett

Latimer Publications

Latimer Briefings

LB01	*The Church of England: What it is, and what it stands for*	R. T. Beckwith
LB02	*Praying with Understanding: Explanations of Words and Passages in the Book of Common Prayer*	R. T. Beckwith
LB03	*The Failure of the Church of England? The Church, the Nation and the Anglican Communion*	A. Pollard
LB04	*Towards a Heritage Renewed*	H.R.M. Craig
LB05	*Christ's Gospel to the Nations: The Heart & Mind of Evangelicalism Past, Present & Future*	Peter Jensen
LB06	*Passion for the Gospel: Hugh Latimer (1485–1555) Then and Now. A commemorative lecture to mark the 450th anniversary of his martyrdom in Oxford*	A. McGrath
LB07	*Truth and Unity in Christian Fellowship*	Michael Nazir-Ali
LB08	*Unworthy Ministers: Donatism and Discipline Today*	Mark Burkill
LB09	*Witnessing to Western Muslims: A Worldview Approach to Sharing Faith*	Richard Shumack
LB10	*Scarf or Stole at Ordination? A Plea for the Evangelical Conscience*	Andrew Atherstone
LB11	*How to Write a Theology Essay*	Michael P. Jensen
LB12	*Preaching: A Guidebook for Beginners*	Allan Chapple
LB13	*Justification by Faith: Orientating the Church's teaching and practice to Christ (Toon Lecture 1)*	Michael Nazir-Ali
LB14	*"Remember Your Leaders": Principles and Priorities for Leaders from Hebrews 13*	Wallace Benn
LB15	*How the Anglican Communion came to be and where it is going*	Michael Nazir-Ali
LB16	*Divine Allurement: Cranmer's Comfortable Words*	Ashley Null
LB17	*True Devotion: In Search of Authentic Spirituality*	Allan Chapple
LB18	*Commemorating War and Praying for Peace: A Christian reflection on the Armed Forces*	John Neal

Anglican Foundations Series

FWC	*The Faith We Confess: An Exposition of the 39 Articles*	Gerald Bray
AF02	*The 'Very Pure Word of God': The Book of Common Prayer as a Model of Biblical Liturgy*	Peter Adam
AF03	*Dearly Beloved: Building God's People Through Morning and Evening Prayer*	Mark Burkill
AF04	*Day by Day: The Rhythm of the Bible in the Book of Common Prayer*	Benjamin Sargent
AF05	*The Supper: Cranmer and Communion*	Nigel Scotland
AF06	*A Fruitful Exhortation: A Guide to the Homilies*	Gerald Bray
AF07	*Instruction in the Way of the Lord: A Guide to the Prayer Book Catechism*	Martin Davie
AF08	*Till Death Us Do Part: "The Solemnization of Matrimony" in the Book of Common Prayer*	Simon Vibert
AF09	*'Sure and Certain Hope': Death and Burial in the Book of Common Prayer*	Andrew Cinnamond

Latimer Publications

Latimer Books

GGC	*God, Gays and the Church: Human Sexuality and Experience in Christian Thinking*	eds. Lisa Nolland, Chris Sugden, Sarah Finch
WTL	*The Way, the Truth and the Life: Theological Resources for a Pilgrimage to a Global Anglican Future*	eds. Vinay Samuel, Chris Sugden, Sarah Finch
AEID	*Anglican Evangelical Identity – Yesterday and Today*	J.I.Packer, N.T.Wright
IB	*The Anglican Evangelical Doctrine of Infant Baptism*	John Stott, Alec Motyer
BF	*Being Faithful: The Shape of Historic Anglicanism Today*	Theological Resource Group of GAFCON
TPG	*The True Profession of the Gospel: Augustus Toplady and Reclaiming our Reformed Foundations*	Lee Gatiss
SG	*Shadow Gospel: Rowan Williams and the Anglican Communion Crisis*	Charles Raven
TTB	*Translating the Bible: From William Tyndale to King James*	Gerald Bray
PWS	*Pilgrims, Warriors, and Servants: Puritan Wisdom for Today's Church*	ed. Lee Gatiss
PPA	*Preachers, Pastors, and Ambassadors: Puritan Wisdom for Today's Church*	ed. Lee Gatiss
CWP	*The Church, Women Bishops and Provision: The Integrity of Orthodox Objections to the Proposed Legislation Allowing Women Bishops*	
TSF	*The Truth Shall Set You Free: Global Anglicans in the 21st Century*	ed. Charles Raven
LMM	*Launching Marsden's Mission: The Beginnings of the Church Missionary Society in New Zealand, viewed from New South Wales*	eds. Peter G Bolt David B. Pettett
MST1	*Listen To Him: Reading and Preaching Emmanuel in Matthew*	Ed. Peter Bolt
GWC	*The Genius of George Whitefield: Reflections on his Ministry from 21st Century Africa*	Ed. Benjamin Dean & Adriaan Neele